White Grass Cafe

Cross Country Cooking

Laurie Little and Mary Beth Gwyer

Illustrations by Mary Ann Yarsinske and Chris Leon

International Standard Book Number 0-87012-570-2
Library of Congress Catalog Card Number 96-095192
Printed in the United States of America
Copyright © 1996 by
White Grass Ski Touring Center
HC 70 Box 299
Davis, WV 26260
304-866-4114
www.whitegrass.com
(e-mail) chip@whitegrass.com
All Rights Reserved

1st Printing - 1996
2nd Printing - 1997
3rd Printing - 2000
4th Printing - 2001
5th Printing - 2004

Master-Craft Printers
100 East Liberty Street
Oakland, MD 21550-1202
2004

This book is lovingly dedicated to all those

who have taught, helped and inspired us.

Thank You, Thank You, Thank You.

Ski Touring Center

Introduction

An exceptional amount of snowfall brought Chip Chase and Winslow Ayer to Canaan Valley, WV in 1980. Their love for cross country and telemark skiing inspired them to bring groups of people from White Grass Knob, to Canaan to ski. The original White Grass began in a one-room nordic schoolhouse near Criders, VA, in the Shenandoah Mountains. Bill Moore, a friend and then naturalist of Canaan Valley State Park, introduced them to the old Weiss Knob Ski Area nearby. The old abandoned lodge was once run by Bob and Anita Barton in the late 1950's and was an early favorite of the Washington Ski Club. Old leather ski boots, wooden skis and a pot bellied stove were all that remained.

An agreement was made with farm owner Randall Reed; renovations of the old lodge began and White Grass Ski Touring was born. Since then, White Grass has grown to be one of the most popular ski touring centers in the East. The same love for the outdoors and the cross country skiing spirit remains strong and true today.

I was lured to the mountain valley by the chance to work at a nearby riding stable; myself not yet a cross country skier. Winslow, Chip and I lived inside the lodge while renovating it, (with a lot of help from our friends.) Chip and I were married and continued to live at White Grass until our first son, Cory, was ten months old. Then, we settled into the caretaker's house on the Reed farm.

The conception of the cafe came from Mary Ann Yarsinske. She knew good food complemented the ski touring scene, and that those cross country skiers could work up some appetites. Soups, sandwiches and incredible cookies, breads and cakes were the original fare. The kitchen started out very simple, with a wood stove for all meal preparation and hot water.

All those who were drawn to Mary Ann's idea are considered co-creators of the whole foods cafe. We all learned from each other. Over the years, while I had babies, Charlie Waters and Colleen Laffey pulled us through with incredible meals. Tom Yocum cooked during one of the worst snow years in our 15 year history, (we ate well anyway).

When Mary Beth Gwyer appeared one weekend from Richmond,VA, just to ski, she was lured to the kitchen by... probably a chocolate chip cookie or a brownie. She has been here since 1992 and has made the cafe stand on its own with great cooking talent.

Our idea to do this cook book has been brewing for over three years now and has finally shown its face to become a reality. We give you the best of what we make, so you can enjoy the same at home.

We wish you simplicity and health in your life!

Laurie Little

WHITE GRASS TOURING CENTER

"I often hear people refer to Canaan as a place with a lot of potential, which I would agree with. However, I believe Canaan's greatest potential has already been realized...Canaan is a place to simply enjoy. To me, nothing represents that "laid back" attitude better than that little barn with gravel floors, chairs that don't match, and that little guy with the big grin. That place is "White Grass.""

Brian J. Hart

White Grass Haiku
By Jim Crutchfield, et. al.

Wooden
Skis
Gentle Snow
Falls Soft
Cold Windows
Hot Chocolate
Friends Talking
Peaceful
Soft Music
White Grass

White Grass Cafe
Freeland Road - Canaan Valley, WV 866-4114

This is a collection of our favorite and most popular foods that we have made throughout the years. Many are generous contributions from friends and family.

Lots of good energy has gone into preparing wholesome and delicious foods for many people. Enjoy these recipes with the ones you love.

Table of Contents

Food For Thought...

Life is short, so eat for body,
soul and mind (and tastebuds.)
Whole foods cooking is the most
flavorful and nutritious way to
nourish ourselves. High fiber,
lots of veggies and plenty of
exercise (like cross country
skiing) are our recipe for
feeling great.

APPETIZERS

Our appetizers are simple to make and
unforgettable in flavor.

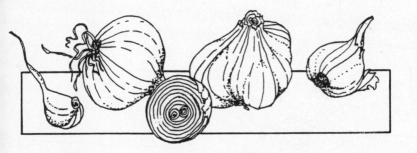

SPINACH DIP

The flavor of this dip improves with age, so make it the day before serving. It is best served in a hollowed-out round loaf of bread. Tear up pieces of bread for dipping. Then eat the bowl after all the dip is gone.

1 10 oz. pkg. frozen spinach
1 16 oz. container of sour cream
1 clove garlic, minced
1 Tbs. onion, finely minced
1 tsp. dried basil
1 tsp. seasoned salt
1/4 tsp. black pepper

Thaw spinach and cook in microwave according to package directions. Cool and squeeze out all excess water. In a large bowl, add all ingredients and mix very well. Adjust seasoning to taste.

HOT BEAN DIP

This is an excellent last minute hot hors d'oeuvre and a great filling for bean burritos. You may want to double the recipe.

    3 cloves garlic, chopped
    1 medium onion, chopped
    1/2 cup chopped green pepper
    1 Tbs. vegetable oil
    1 can refried beans or
        2 cups cooked pinto beans
    1 cup shredded Cheddar cheese
    1 tsp. hot sauce or spicy salsa

In a saucepan, sauté garlic, onion and green pepper in oil, over medium heat until tender. Add beans and cheese. Stir until cheese has thoroughly melted. Add hot sauce and serve with tortilla chips.

HUMMUS

Next to our homemade chili and soups, this is one of the most famous White Grass lunch favorites.

2 cups well cooked garbanzo beans (very soft)
1/4 cup tahini (sesame butter)
4 Tbs. lemon juice
3 cloves chopped garlic
1 Tbs. chopped fresh parsley
2 Tbs. water
2 tsp. olive oil
Salt and pepper to taste

Puree all ingredients in a food processor. Serve as a dip with warm pita wedges or spread on bread. Fill a pocket sandwich with lettuce and fresh veggies (carrots, olives, cucumbers, tomatoes, onions, sprouts, chopped green onions, feta cheese, etc).

SMOKED TROUT DIP

1 8 oz. pkg. flaked smoked trout*
1 8 oz. sour cream
1/2 tsp. ground cumin
Juice from 1/2 lemon
1 Tbs. horseradish

Pick through the trout and check for stray bones. Mix all ingredients well, refrigerate and serve with good quality crackers or pita wedges.

*Living in the mountains of West Virginia, we at White Grass are surrounded by trout farms. There is never a shortage of fresh fish. We buy packaged smoked trout from Mountain Aquaculture and Producers Association (MA & PA). The cheese ball recipe below is courtesy of of MA & PA. For more information, see page 190.

 ## SMOKED TROUT CHEESE BALL

1/4 lb. smoked trout
8 oz. cream cheese, softened
1 Tbs. horseradish
1 Tbs. grated onion
1 Tbs. lemon juice
3 Tbs. parsley
1/2 cup chopped pecans

Combine first six ingredients, mix well. Place in plastic wrap and roll into a ball. Remove and roll in nuts. Chill and serve with crackers.

BALO de QUESO
(Cheese Ball)

Some people think cheese balls are pretty "ho hum". This one is exceptional, so we gave it a more exciting name.

2　8 oz. pkgs. cream cheese
2　Tbs. finely chopped onion
2　Tbs. carrot, chopped
2　Tbs. celery, chopped
2　Tbs. horseradish
1/4　cup mayonnaise
1/3　cup Parmesan cheese
1/2　tsp. salt
3/4　cup chopped nuts

Let cream cheese soften to room temperature. In a food processor, finely chop onion, carrot and celery. Then add remaining ingredients.

Form a ball and roll in chopped nuts (pecans, walnuts, or almonds), then roll in plastic wrap. Refrigerate and serve with crackers.

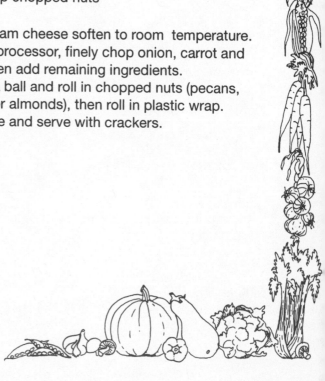

TAPENADE
(OLIVE SPREAD)

It is important to use Calamata, Nicoise or other imported olives. Plain canned black olives will not do this recipe justice.

- 1 cup Calamata olives, pitted
- 4 cloves garlic, chopped
- 1 Tbs. olive oil
- 1 Tbs. fresh lemon juice

Combine olives and garlic in a food processor and process until it forms a paste. While the machine is running, slowly pour in the olive oil, then the lemon juice.

Spoon into a beautiful bowl and serve with warm pita wedges or bagel crisps. This is also a delicious spread on your favorite sandwich. Makes 1 cup.

Our friend and former cafe cook, Charlie Waters, inspired this easy and elegant appetizer. She is a fabulous cook and a great telemark instructor, among other things.

PICKLED SHRIMP

This is an elegant appetizer with a lemon butter taste.

    2 pounds large green shrimp
    1 1/2 Tbs. seafood seasoning (Old Bay)
    1 cup vegetable oil
    3/4 cup white vinegar
    1 tsp. black peppercorns
    1 Tbs. sugar
    1 tsp. salt
    2 medium onions, sliced extremely thin
    2 lemons, sliced extremely thin
    8 whole bay leaves
    1/4 cup chopped fresh parsley
    1/4 tsp. dried tarragon (optional)

Peel and devein shrimp, leaving only the tails on. Cook shrimp until pink in 2 quarts boiling water and seafood seasoning – don't overcook! Cool immediately and set aside.

In a large glass bowl, add the remaining ingredients and stir. Toss shrimp into the marinade and place in the fridge for at least two hours and serve. It's best not to marinate shrimp overnight, they begin to disintegrate after too long.

SPINACH BALLS

This is a great party snack that can be made ahead of time. You can also make delicious stuffed mushrooms -- just make half a recipe of filling, stuff into caps and bake.

2 10 oz. packages frozen chopped spinach
1 medium onion, finely chopped
2 1/2 cups Pepperidge Farm Seasoned Stuffing
1/4 cup butter or margarine
1-1/2 cups Parmesan cheese
6 eggs
Salt and pepper to taste

Thaw spinach and squeeze out all excess water. Mix all ingredients and form into small balls. Bake at 350° for 15 minutes. Serve immediately. Uncooked spinach balls can be frozen on a sheet and thawed when needed for baking.

This recipe is from Janet Moore, Chip's sister, who
lives in Bennington, Vermont.

MEXICAN ROLLUPS

Serve these at your next gathering and they will be a smashing success. If you have any leftover filling, plop a dollup on a baked potato and add some salsa – you'll have a Mexican Baked Potato – delish.

    1 8 oz. package cream cheese
    1 bunch green onions, chopped
    1 10 oz. can black olives
    1 dozen flour tortillas
    1 cup White Grass Salsa

Let cream cheese soften at room temperature for at least an hour. Then combine cream cheese, onions and olives in a food processor until smooth. Spread mixture evenly over each flour tortilla (not too thick). Roll tortilla and cut into 1 inch pieces. Arrange on a platter and serve with a bowl of homemade salsa, see page 22.

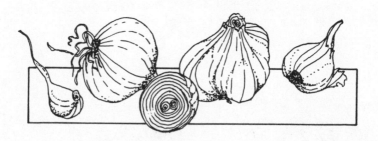

A very dear lifelong friend, Shannon Huennekens Mitchell, gave me this recipe. Who at St. Gertrude High would have ever dreamed she would become a domestic goddess? MBG

CAJUN SHRIMP ROLLUPS

1/2 lb. raw shrimp, peeled and deveined
2 Tbs. Cajun seasoning (see page 143)
1/2 Tbs. oil
3 cloves garlic, minced
1 8 oz. cream cheese, softened
1 carrot, peeled and chopped
1 small onion, chopped
2 Tbs. fresh chopped parsley
1 large package flour tortillas

Mix Cajun seasoning with shrimp and marinate in a bowl at least 1/2 hour. Then sauté garlic in oil for 1 minute and add shrimp, stirring, and cook until tender – don't overcook.

In a food processor, blend cream cheese, carrots, onion and parsley. Remove from processor and mix cream cheese mixture with shrimp (you may want to first cut the shrimp into smaller pieces). Spread a light layer of filling over each flour tortilla and roll – cut into pieces. The rollups are then ready to serve room temperature or chilled. They're to die for.

21

WHITE GRASS SALSA

Another of our most famous and easy recipes. You'll never buy another jar at the store after making and tasting this.

One 28 oz. can good quality tomatoes, chopped
1/2 onion, chopped
3 green onions, chopped
1/2 green bell pepper, chopped
1 small jalapeno pepper, seeded and chopped
2 cloves garlic, minced
1 tsp. ground cumin
1/2 tsp. black pepper
2 tsp. fresh parsley or cilantro, chopped

Stir all ingredients together. Cover and refrigerate. Salsa is better after spices marry. This will keep in the fridge for up to two weeks. If you don't have a jalapeno pepper, substitute 1/4 tsp. of cayenne pepper.

In the spring, we jazz up this recipe by adding ramps instead of green onions. Ramps are a pungent wild leek that grow in West Virginia. Every year, we look forward to their arrival and the Ramp festivals and dinners that follow.

E-Z GUACAMOLE

2 ripe avocados (soft)
Juice from 1 lemon or 1 lime
2 Tbs. homemade salsa

Cut avocados in half and scoop out the meat. Smash with a fork, then add juice and salsa – mix and eat. Now that's easy! Serves 4.

GUACAMOLE

2 ripe avocados (soft)
2 Tbs. finely chopped onion
Juice from 1 lemon or 1 lime
1 small tomato, finely chopped
2 cloves garlic, minced
1 small jalapeno, seeded and chopped or
   a dash or two of your favorite hot sauce

Scoop out avocados, mash and stir in remaining ingredients. Mix well and enjoy. Serve with fajitas or alone with corn chips. Serves 4.

QUESADILLAS

Basically, this is a warm Mexican sandwich – two flour tortillas with melted cheese and whatnot in between.

Lay one flour tortilla in a heated cast iron or heavy skillet. Cover it with your choice of cheese, vegetable, fruit, meat, etc. Top with another flour tortilla. Turn the whole thing over, gently, and warm it on the other side until tortilla lightly browns. Cut into quarters and serve. Kids love them!

Our favorite quesadilla fillings:

Cheddar cheese	guacamole
sliced tomatoes	salsa
fresh spinach	goat cheese
bean sprouts	Monterey Jack
sliced apples	black beans
refried beans	roasted red peppers*
cream cheese	green chilies

*HOW TO ROAST PEPPERS

Roasted peppers give a rich and smoky flavor to any dish. You can roast any type of pepper; red or green bell, ancho, jalapeno or chile, for instance.

To roast peppers, place whole pepper directly on a gas burner and turn, occasionally, until pepper is blistery and black. Place peppers in a paper bag for 15 minutes. Peel off black skin and rinse. Peppers are then ready to eat.

If using an electric oven, slice peppers in half and lay on a baking sheet. Broil until black and continue with other directions.

VEGGIE STUFFED MUSHROOMS

1 onion, chopped
3 cloves garlic, minced
1 Tbs. olive oil
1 carrot, peeled and finely chopped
2 Tbs. roasted red pepper, chopped
1 small zucchini or squash, finely chopped
1 lb. large fresh mushrooms
2 Tbs. fresh parsley, chopped
3 Tbs. dry white wine
1 tsp. Worchestershire sauce
Parmesan cheese

Sauté onion and garlic in oil for two minutes. Then add carrots and squash, cook another few minutes. Remove stems from mushrooms and chop and add them to the skillet. Finally, add parsley, wine and Worchestershire. Cook for two minutes. Spoon filling into each mushroom cap and sprinkle with Parmesan. Bake for 20 minutes at 350°, serve immediately.

This is a slight variation of my brother David's recipe. (Everyone in my family cooks.) He doesn't add carrot and squash to his mushrooms, but I just like to "beef up" the vegetable content. They're delicious either way you make them. MBG

FRUIT SALSA

1 medium red onion
1/2 orange, peeled or
  1 11 oz. can mandarin oranges, drained
2 cloves garlic
1 jalapeno pepper
1/2 mango
1/2 cup fresh cilantro
1 roasted red pepper*
1 small pickling cucumber, peeled
Juice from 1 lime

Finely chop all ingredients and mix together in a bowl with lime juice. Let sit at least two hours before serving. This will last for days in the fridge.

This is quite a different type of salsa and can be made in different ways. You can substitute any of the ingredients for anything you like, depending on your taste:

| apples | strawberry | kiwi |
| plums | parsley | corn |

Serve fruit salsa with grilled chicken or fish, baked garlic bread, corn cakes or chips.

* See page 24 for pepper roasting directions.

SOUPS

Soups are a mainstay of our cafe and our lives. Nothing seems to warm your heart and soul more on a cold day. Our soups, made from scratch, can never compare to can or mix soups.

Love Letters

Neither of us dreamed that in four years we would have 5,000 copies of this cookbook in print! Thanks to all who have supported us. We'd like to share some of our favorite letters we've received, Laurie and M.B.

"I feel as though I have found a good friend! White Grass Cafe Cookbook is one of the most functional cookbooks I have used. The recipes are delectable, healthy and easy to prepare... As a proponent of quick and nutritious foods, I would give this cookbook my highest recommendation."
Anne Harris
Taftsville, VT

"The cookbook captures the style of White Grass and allows one to get a taste of the cafe during those 8 months out of the year when it is closed. This book has some great recipes- they're easy to follow and taste fabulous."
"Laid Back Gourmet"
Washington, DC

"The White Grass Cafe may only be open 4 months each winter but our WGC Cookbook is open at least once a week."
John & Martha Mueller
Boston, MA

"Never used a cookbook so much. It makes me feel like I'm back in WV. It's truly wonderful. Thanks for being my cooking teachers."
Deb Klein
New York

MAKING STOCK

The key to good soup is a good stock. We make our own. It is easy to make a vegetable stock. Just take any or all of the following and cook for at least 20 minutes in a large pot of water. Strain and use in your favorite soup:

> scraps of clean vegetable peelings
> spinach stems
> carrot ends and peels
> onion skins and stems
> mushroom stems
> parsley stems
> celery ends
> potato water

(Some vegetables like broccoli and cauliflower make stock bitter and should not be used.)

In many of our recipes, we use Vegetable Broth Powder. It is a blend of herbs and seasonings used to flavor soups, stocks or sauces. It can be purchased from your local health food store. Use it whenever you think your broth needs extra seasoning. You may always substitute boullion for broth powder.

CURRIED SWEET POTATO SOUP

4 medium orange fleshed sweet potatoes
2 1/2 cups water or stock
2 Tbs. butter
1 medium onion, chopped
2 cloves garlic, minced
1 tsp. cinnamon
1 tsp. ground cumin
1/4 tsp. dry mustard
3/4 tsp. ground ginger
Dash of cayenne pepper
1/2 tsp. coriander
1 6 oz. can frozen orange juice concentrate
Juice from 1 lemon

Peel sweet potatoes and cut into 1-inch cubes. In a soup pot, boil sweet potatoes in water or stock until cooked. Drain potatoes and save liquid.

While potatoes are cooking, sauté onion and garlic in butter until soft, add spices and stir.

Puree potatoes and onion/spice mixture in a food processor, return to the pot and add orange juice concentrate and enough potato stock to reach desired thickness. Stir in lemon juice. Let simmer 5 - 15 minutes before serving. A dollup of yogurt is a superb garnish for this soup.

Ruth Fleischman Melnick, one of our "Soup Queens",
made this superb soup during one of our busiest,
snowiest seasons. It was a hit.

MEDITERRANEAN CHICK PEA SOUP

Another of Ruth Fleischman Melnick's fabulous soups. It's spicy, so make it on an extra cold day.

3 Tbs. olive oil
1 large onion, chopped
3 cloves garlic, minced
3 carrots, peeled and chopped
1 stalk celery, chopped
3 cups water or stock
1 tsp. cinnamon
1/8 tsp. cayenne pepper
2 tsp. paprika
1 tsp. turmeric
1 tsp. salt
1 tsp. dried basil
1 bay leaf
1 cup fresh tomatoes, chopped, or
   1 28 oz. can diced tomatoes
1 16 oz. can chick peas, rinsed and drained

In a large saucepan, sauté onion and garlic in oil for two minutes. Add carrots and celery, cook another 2 - 3 minutes. Add water or stock and spices. Simmer over med-low heat and add tomatoes and chick peas. Allow soup to simmer over low heat for 20 - 30 minutes. Enjoy.

ITALIAN VEGETABLE AND RICE SOUP

1 large can tomatoes, chopped, with juice
2 quarts vegetable stock
1/2 cup uncooked rice
1 Tbs. olive oil
1 onion, chopped
2 cloves garlic, minced
3 carrots, chopped
1 zucchini, cubed
1 yellow squash, cubed
1 10 oz. pkg. frozen or 2 cups fresh
      green beans
1 tsp. dried basil
1 tsp. dried oregano
1 tsp. dried thyme
1-2 Tbs. vegetable broth powder
Salt* and pepper to taste

In a large soup pot, cook rice with tomatoes and stock over medium heat. In the meantime, sauté onion and garlic in oil for 2 minutes, then add carrots, squash and zucchini – cook until tender. Add veggies to the soup, cook 20 minutes then add green beans and herbs.

Simmer another 15 minutes, or until beans and rice are done. Season with salt and pepper. Serve in gigantic bowls with bread on the side; sprinkle the soup with some Parmesan cheese. Serves 4 - 6.

*Just a reminder - don't over salt your soups! As Laurie's Dad says "You can always add it – but you can't take it out."

MINESTRONE

2 cloves garlic, minced
1 medium onion, chopped
1 Tbs. olive oil
1 carrot, sliced
1 celery stalk, sliced
1 zucchini, sliced
2 potatoes, diced
3 1/2 cups vegetable stock
2 cups Marinara sauce (see page 94)
1 15 oz. can cannellini beans, drained
Pinch of crushed sage
1 tsp. dried basil
3/4 cup frozen peas
1/3 cup small pasta
Salt and pepper to taste

In a large soup pot, sauté garlic and onion in oil for 3 minutes. Add remaining vegetables, stock, sauce, beans and herbs. Let soup simmer 30 minutes. Then add pasta and peas, continue to simmer until pasta is al dente ("to the tooth" meaning firm.) Serve with Parmesan cheese and warm Italian bread. Serves 4 - 6.

FIESTA CHICKEN CHILI

1 cup chopped onion
2 cloves garlic, minced
1 Tbs. oil
3 cups water
1/2 cup pearled barley
1 16 oz. can tomatoes, chopped with liquid
1 16 oz. can tomato puree
2 - 3 cups vegetable or chicken stock
1 cup frozen corn
1/4 cup chopped green chiles
1 Tbs. chili powder
1/2 tsp. ground cumin
1 tsp. salt
1/2 tsp. black pepper
3 cups cooked chicken (about 1 1/2 lbs.)

In a large soup pot, cook onion and garlic in oil until tender. Add remaining ingredients, except for chicken. Bring to a boil, then reduce heat to low and cover. Simmer 40 minutes, stirring occasionally. Add chicken and continue cooking 10 minutes. Add more stock if necessary to thin out. Serves 4 - 6.

WHITE GRASS CHILI
Vegetarian and Delicious

2 1/2 cups dried or two 16 oz. cans pinto beans
2 tsp. salt
2 Tbs. olive oil
2 medium onions, chopped
4 cloves garlic, chopped
3 stalks celery, chopped
4 carrots, peeled and grated
1 large green pepper, chopped
1/3 cup raw bulgur
1 Tbs. ground cumin
1 tsp. dried basil
1 tsp. dried oregano
3 Tbs. chili powder
1/4 tsp. or a dash cayenne pepper
1 16oz. can whole tomatoes, chopped
1 16oz. can tomato puree
Salt and pepper to taste

If using dried beans, soak them overnight in 2 quarts water (plus a dash of baking soda). Rinse and cook in fresh water with the salt. Cook until tender, (about one hour).

In a large saucepan, sauté onion, garlic, celery, carrots, and green pepper in olive oil. Add bulgur, spices, herbs and one cup water. Mix well and add cooked beans, one cup of bean broth, tomatoes and puree. Let simmer 45 minutes or until bulgur is softened. It may be necessary to add more water to determine thickness. Serve topped with grated Jack or Cheddar cheese. Serves 6.

This is by far the most popular dish served at White Grass. We should have a sign reading "Over A Billion Bowls Served".

SPINACH MUSHROOM BARLEY SOUP

3 Tbs. margarine or butter
3/4 cup dry pearled barley
1 large onion, chopped
4 cloves garlic, minced
1/2 lb. fresh mushrooms, sliced
10 cups water
1 tsp. seasoned salt
1/4 cup dry sherry
1 1/2 Tbs. vegetable broth powder
3 Tbs. soy sauce
1/2 lb. fresh spinach, washed and torn in pieces

In a large pot, melt butter and add barley. Toast barley until golden brown (this makes the soup richer). Then add onions and garlic, sauté 4 minutes or until tender. Add mushrooms and cook 3 minutes. Add water and seasoned salt. Cover and let simmer until barley has swelled and thickened, about 45 minutes. Then add soy sauce, sherry, broth powder and spinach. Adjust seasoning and serve. Note: the longer this soup cooks, the thicker it gets. Serves 4 - 6.

What a fabulous soup! Healthy and delicious. You can vary this by adding more garlic (yeah) or substituting spinach for other greens like kale or swiss chard.

VEGETARIAN FRENCH ONION SOUP

4 Tbs. butter
4 large onions, sliced extremely thin
4 cloves garlic, chopped
2-3 Tbs. brown sugar
8 cups vegetable stock (see directions page 29)
1 Tbs. vegetable broth powder
Soy sauce to taste
Dry bread or bread crumbs
provolone or mozzarella cheese sliced

In large soup pot, sauté onion and garlic in butter. When tender, stir in brown sugar and continue to brown (carmelize) onion. Then add stock and vegetable broth powder, stir and simmer at least 30 minutes. Add soy sauce to taste. Serve in a bowl with dry bread and cheese. Heavenly! Serves 4 - 6.

NEW ENGLAND CLAM CHOWDER

For a delicious potato soup, follow these directions, and just leave out the clams. Corn is a good replacement.

2 Tbs. margarine or butter
1 large onion, chopped
2 cloves garlic, chopped
2 ribs celery, chopped
2 carrots, chopped
6 large potatoes, washed and diced
1/2 cup all-purpose flour
1 1/2 tsp. salt
1 tsp. vegetable broth powder
1/4 tsp. black pepper
1/2 gallon milk
1 10 oz. can chopped clams
1 tsp. dried parsley

In heavy bottomed soup pot, sauté onion, garlic, celery and carrots in butter until tender. Add potatoes, sprinkle with flour, salt, pepper and veggie powder, mix. Pour in milk and stir well. Cook on low heat, uncovered, until potatoes are soft. Stir occasionally to keep from sticking. When potatoes are done, add clams and their juice and parsley. Let simmer 10 minutes. Voila!

One of Chip's favorite's, this soup is a popular choice of cross country skiers on a snowy day. And it's even better the next day, (if there is any left.)

POTATO PESTO SOUP

This soup was born one Sunday morning at the cafe when we had an overabundance of pesto. (Too much pesto? Never!) It's such a delicious, versatile condiment. We love pesto.

    2 onions, chopped
    4 cloves garlic, minced
    1 Tbs. butter
    2 ribs celery, chopped
    2 carrots, peeled and chopped
    6 large potatoes, cubed
    8 cups water
    2 Tbs. pesto (see page 106)
    1 tsp. salt
    1/2 tsp. black pepper

In large soup pot, sauté onion and garlic in butter over medium heat. Cook for 2 minutes then add celery and carrots. Pour in water and potatoes. Let soup simmer until potatoes are cooked, about 30 minutes. Then add pesto, salt and pepper. Simmer another 5 minutes, adjust seasonings and serve. Makes 8 servings.

SPLIT PEA SOUP

You'll notice there are no ham bones or jowls in this recipe. We think it is possible to make this soup even more delicious without meat.

1 large onion, chopped
3 cloves garlic, minced
1 Tbs. olive oil
2 carrots, peeled and chopped
2 cups green split peas
8 cups water or stock
1 Tbs. vegetable broth powder
1 tsp. dried thyme
1/4 tsp. black pepper
1/2 tsp. salt

In a large soup pot, sauté onion and garlic in oil until tender. Add carrots, cook another minute. Pour in water or stock and peas and seasonings. Simmer, stirring occasionally, until peas are soft. The longer this soup cooks, the better it tastes. Give it at least 2 hours.

You can excite this recipe by adding fresh or ground ginger or cayenne pepper – give your tastebuds a thrill.

BLACK BEAN SOUP

Serve in a big bowl with a dollup of sour cream and diced green onions on top.

2 cups dried or 2 cans black beans
9 cups water
1 large onion, diced
1 green bell pepper, diced
3 cloves garlic, minced
1 Tbs. olive oil
2 tsp. ground cumin
1/4 tsp. cayenne pepper
1/2 tsp. salt
1/4 tsp. black pepper

If using dried beans, soak overnight in salted water with 1/4 tsp. baking soda. Rinse beans and cover with 9 cups fresh water. Cook beans with 1/2 tsp. salt until tender.

Meanwhile, chop veggies and sauté in olive oil. Add rinsed, drained beans. Puree all ingredients in a food processor and return them to the soup pot. Add seasonings and additional water if too thick. Serves 4 - 6.

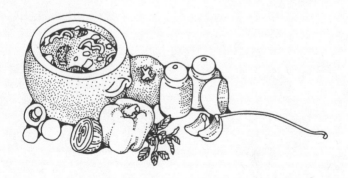

CURRIED LENTIL SOUP

1 Tbs. oil
1 large onion, chopped
2 cloves garlic, chopped
3 carrots, chopped
2 stalks celery, chopped
1 lb. dried lentils
2 quarts stock or water
1 Tbs. vegetable broth powder
2 tsp. curry powder
Dash of cayenne pepper
Seasoned salt to taste

In a large soup pot, sauté onion, garlic, carrot and celery in oil until tender. Then add lentils and cover with stock or water by 2 - 3 inches. Add spices and simmer over med-low heat until lentils are tender (about one hour). Stir occasionally and adjust seasoning if needed. You may add water if more broth is desired. Serves 4 - 6.

> Tom Yocum, former cafe cook and staff comedian, used to serve this over mashed potatoes. He called it "Dal Potot".

CLOUD SOUP

This is navy bean soup traditionally made with a ham bone stock, but I've created a vegetarian version. I always called the dumplings "clouds" as a kid. This is an adaptation of a recipe from my grandmother, Agnes Little. LKL

2 cups dry navy beans
3 quarts water or stock
1/2 tsp. salt
1 onion, chopped
2 cloves garlic, minced
1 Tbs. butter
1 Tbs. vegetable broth powder
1/4 tsp. white pepper
1 cup Bisquick
1/3 cup milk

Soak beans in water overnight (add 1/2 tsp. baking soda to help prevent gas). Rinse and cook in fresh water and salt. Add more water while cooking if needed. You need to make sure there is plenty of broth for steaming dumplings.

In a skillet, sauté onion and garlic in butter and add to the beans. Add veggie broth powder and pepper; let soup simmer one hour. When beans are cooked, add dumplings.

For the dumplings, stir Bisquick and milk until a soft dough forms. Drop by rounded spoonfuls into boiling soup. Dumplings float to top when cooked. I like them a little soft and they help thicken the broth. If you like, add fresh chopped parsley and add salt to taste.

TOMATO BISQUE

This recipe is from Patty Loebig, mother of a dear friend. Blending the flour and milk makes this soup thick but also light - you'll see what we mean.

1 large onion, sliced
2 cloves garlic, minced
2 Tbs. butter
2 Tbs. olive oil
4 cups diced fresh tomatoes or
     canned tomatoes
1/2 tsp. dried basil
1/4 tsp. black pepper
1/2 tsp. dried thyme
1 tsp. salt
3 Tbs. tomato paste
2 cups broth
1 tsp. sugar
2 Tbs. flour
2 cups non fat milk or evaporated skim milk

BASIL

Sauté onions and garlic in butter and oil in a soup pot. Cook 4 minutes, add tomatoes and spices, stir, then add broth (chicken or vegetable), tomato paste and sugar. Simmer for 20 minutes. Remove from heat and pureé in a blender or food processor and pour back into the saucepan. Mix milk and flour in the blender and stir into the tomato mixture. Simmer 10 minutes and serve. Serves 6.

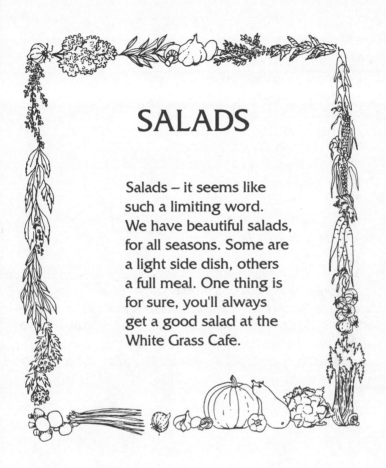

SALADS

Salads – it seems like
such a limiting word.
We have beautiful salads,
for all seasons. Some are
a light side dish, others
a full meal. One thing is
for sure, you'll always
get a good salad at the
White Grass Cafe.

BETSY'S TOMATO SALAD

3 - 4 red, ripe summer tomatoes, sliced
1 thin sliced sweet onion
1/4 tsp. dried basil
1/4 tsp. dried oregano
1/4 tsp. dried dill
1/4 tsp. dried chives
1/2 tsp. sugar
2 tsp. red wine vinegar or lemon juice
2 Tbs. olive oil
1 clove garlic, minced
1/8 tsp. black pepper

Start a layer of tomatoes in a shallow glass pan. Then add a sprinkle of seasonings (and sugar) over the top. Make a marinade by mixing vinegar, olive oil, garlic and pepper. Sprinkle a little marinade over the tomatoes. Then add a layer of onion. Continue the layering process, cover and chill for 2 hours before serving. The juices and marinade create the most wonderful flavor. Makes 4 - 6 servings.

A summertime delight from our friend,
Betsy Reed, owner of Canaan Realty.

CUCUMBERS IN SOUR CREAM

This is a fabulous summer garden dish – and very easy too.

4 - 6 pickling cucumbers
1/2 of a medium onion
1 tsp. salt
1/4 tsp. black pepper
1/4 cup sour cream
1/4 tsp. dried dill weed (optional)

Peel and slice cucumbers and onion, very thin, and put them in bowl. Generously sprinkle with salt and let set 30 minutes. Then squeeze out excess water, return to the bowl and stir in sour cream and dill. Add pepper and serve.

ALMOND RAISIN CHICKEN SALAD

4 chicken breasts
1/3 cup raisins
1 2.5 pkg. sliced almonds
1/2 cup mayonnaise
salt and pepper to taste

Boil chicken in a large pot of water until cooked and tender, about 20 minutes. Don't overcook or it will be tough. While meat is cooling, spread almonds out on a cookie sheet and toast in a 375° oven for 5 minutes. Keep an eye on them so they don't burn.

Meanwhile, tear chicken meat into chunks. Mix chicken, raisins, almonds and mayo and season. Serve on a croissant or whole grain bun. This salad is equally delicious served on a bed of lettuce with fresh grapes. Serves 4.

ORIENTAL CHICKEN SALAD

1 head leaf or romaine lettuce
2 cups cooked chicken, shredded
1 carrot, grated
1/2 cup red bell pepper, chopped
1 cup sliced mushrooms
1 cup fresh bean sprouts
1/4 cup green onions, chopped
1/3 cup roasted sunflower seeds
Anything else you like on a salad
Sesame Garlic Dressing (below)

Wash lettuce and tear into pieces. Arrange lettuce on 4 plates and layer carrot, pepper, mushrooms, sprouts, onions, chicken and sunnies. Have salad dressing on hand and enjoy your meal. Serve with soup and bread.

SESAME GARLIC DRESSING

1/2 cup cider vinegar
1/3 cup vegetable oil
2 tsp. toasted sesame oil
3 Tbs. soy sauce or tamari
1 Tbs. sugar
1 Tbs. lemon juice
1 Tbs. fresh ginger, grated
1 clove garlic, minced

Combine all ingredients in a jar and shake well. Serve immediately or store in refrigerator for up to two weeks.

We serve this at our restaurant. It's our most popular salad dressing,

48

YUM TUNA

1 cup sugar
3/4 cup white or cider vinegar
1/4 cup diced red onion
1/4 cup chopped green onions
1/3 cup chopped peanuts
1/4 cup fresh ginger, julienned
1 Tbs. fresh cilantro, chopped
Crushed dried chile peppers, to taste
2 6 1/2 oz. cans tuna, drained

Cook sugar and vinegar in a small saucepan over medium heat until sugar dissolves. Set aside to cool.

Mix together remaining ingredients, toss with the sauce and refrigerate. Serve on a bed of lettuce. Serves 4 - 6.

Our friend, Anne Weatherford, gave us this incredible recipe. It goes well with Pad Thai, see page 111.

CAESAR SALAD

1 large head romaine lettuce
1 2 oz. can anchovy fillets, drained
1 Tbs. sugar
3 Tbs. red wine vinegar
Juice from one lemon
4 cloves garlic, minced
1/4 cup olive oil
1/2 cup fresh grated Parmesan cheese
Fresh ground black pepper
1 cup croutons

Separate lettuce leaves; wash well and set aside to drain. Mash anchovies with a fork in a flat bowl until they are paste-like. Combine sugar, vinegar, lemon juice, garlic, oil and anchovies in a jar and shake very well. In your most beautiful large serving bowl, tear lettuce into bite-sized pieces. Toss with Parmesan, salad dressing and black pepper. Sprinkle croutons on top and serve immediately. Serves 4 - 6. Try this salad with sliced fresh mushrooms and cherry tomatoes.

I had to "steal" this dressing recipe from my good friends, Jenny and Chris Laude. When they first made it for me, I winced at the can of anchovies, but when I tasted it, I fell in love. Now, I always have a jar of this dressing in my fridge.
MBG

MARINATED VEGETABLE SALAD

1 large yellow squash
1 large zucchini
1 red bell pepper
1 green bell pepper
1 medium red onion
1 pint cherry tomatoes, halved
8 oz. fresh mushrooms, quartered
1 large head romaine lettuce
1 recipe Greek Salad Dressing, (see page 58)

Slice squash, zucchini, peppers and onion into bite-sized pieces. Place in a bowl and cover with salad dressing. Let marinate at least 5 hours in the fridge or overnight.

The mushrooms and tomatoes are more delicate, so let them marinate an hour before serving. Toss torn romaine leaves at the last minute and you are ready to eat. Serves 6 as a side dish.

This is a very easy and delicious dish. You can experiment by adding different things like cauliflower, broccoli, olives, cukes, etc. Even cooked beans like chick peas are good in this salad.

TABOULI

Prepare this dish at least three hours before serving to allow it to thoroughly marinate.

1 cup dry wheat bulgur
1 1/2 cups boiling water*
1 tsp. salt
1/4 cup lemon juice (fresh)
2 cloves garlic, minced
1/2 tsp. dry mint
2 Tbs. olive oil
Dash of black pepper
2 medium tomatoes, chopped
  or 1 14 oz. can tomatoes, chopped
1 cup chopped fresh parsley
1 carrot, grated
1 green bell pepper, chopped
1 cucumber, peeled and chopped
1/2 cup cooked garbanzo beans (optional)

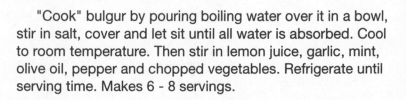

"Cook" bulgur by pouring boiling water over it in a bowl, stir in salt, cover and let sit until all water is absorbed. Cool to room temperature. Then stir in lemon juice, garlic, mint, olive oil, pepper and chopped vegetables. Refrigerate until serving time. Makes 6 - 8 servings.

*Substitute part tomato juice from canned tomatoes when swelling bulgur for added flavor.

VEGETABLE BIRIYANI
An Indian Rice Salad

1 1/2 cups basmati rice
4 bay leaves
1/2 tsp. salt
1 medium onion, diced
2 large carrots, diced
1/2 cup raisins
1 cup cooked chick peas
1/2 cup chopped cilantro

1 cup frozen peas
4 cloves garlic, minced
1 Tbs. vegetable oil
1 Tbs. curry powder
1/4 tsp. cinnamon
1/4 tsp. ground cardamom
1/4 tsp. ground cloves
1/4 tsp. turmeric

In a saucepan, place rice, salt, bay leaves and 3 cups water. Cook over medium heat 15 minutes, then add carrots and onions and continue cooking until rice is tender. Spoon into a large bowl and add raisins, chick peas, cilantro and peas, let cool.

In a skillet, heat oil and sauté garlic for one or two minutes. Add spices, sauté another minute and add 1/3 cup water. Stir well and gently fold spices into rice until well mixed. Add a little cayenne if you like heat. Serves 6 generously.

This incredibly tasty salad is fabulous served warm or cold. It can stand on its own as an entrée or is an excellent side dish.

NICOISE POTATO SALAD

3 pounds small red potatoes
4 green onions, chopped
3 Tbs. fresh parsley, chopped
2 cups fresh green beans, cooked
1/2 pint cherry tomatoes, halved
3/4 cup Calamata olives, pitted
1/2 tsp. dried dill
1/2 cup Lemon Vinaigrette

Slice potatoes in 1/8" rounds and boil until tender. Do not over cook. Mushy potatoes will not hold up in this salad. Drain and cool under cold running water. In a large bowl, gently toss potatoes, onions, parsley, beans, tomatoes, olives and dill. Pour in Lemon Vinaigrette, mix and serve. This salad will keep overnight in the fridge but is best served immediately.

LEMON VINAIGRETTE

1/2 cup olive oil
1/4 cup red wine vinegar
1/4 cup fresh lemon juice
3 cloves garlic, minced
2 tsp. sugar

Mix all ingredients in a jar and shake well. Store in refrigerator until needed. Use this dressing anytime on your favorite salad.

POTATO SALAD

4 lbs. red potatoes with skins on
1 bunch green onions, chopped
1 tsp. celery seed
1/2 tsp. dried dill or 1/4 tsp. fresh dill
Salt and pepper to taste
1 cup mayonnaise
2 Tbs. red wine vinegar
1 Tbs. sugar
1/4 cup chopped fresh parsley

Cut potatoes into cubes and boil until tender in a large pot, about 15 minutes. Don't let the potatoes get too mushy. Drain and cool potatoes (by running cold water over them) and place them in a large bowl. (Save that potato water for soup stock.) Add onions, celery seed, dill, salt and pepper.

In a small bowl, mix mayo, vinegar and sugar. You may want to adjust to your own taste. When the dressing is perfect, add to the salad. Toss gently and garnish with chopped parsley. Serves 6.

> There are a million ways to make potato salad. I like it simple and warm. My mother always adds hard-boiled eggs, fresh chopped celery and garnishes with paprika. Some people like mustard or pickle relish in theirs. Just about any combination makes a good potato salad. MBG

TORTELLINI SALAD

1 pkg. cheese tortellini (1 lb.)
1 cup frozen peas, thawed
1 carrot, grated
1/3 cup grated red cabbage
1/2 tsp. dried dill weed
3/4 cup Raspberry Vinaigrette dressing

Cook tortellini according to package directions. Then run under cold water to cool. In a large bowl, toss all ingredients. Makes 6-8 servings.

RASPBERRY VINAIGRETTE

1/3 cup raspberry vinegar
1 tsp. salt
1 tsp. dry mustard
3/4 cup vegetable oil
1/3 cup sugar
1 1/2 tsp. poppy seed

Combine all ingredients except poppy seed and beat with a whisk until well blended. Add poppy seed. Refrigerate until needed. This dressing is also delicious on your favorite tossed salad.

White Grass Cafe

MYRA'S MARINATED SEASHELLS

12 oz. medium seashell pasta
1/2 cup sugar
3/4 cup red wine or white vinegar
1 11 oz. can tomato soup
2 Tbs. canola or olive oil
Salt and pepper to taste
1 bell pepper, chopped
1 medium onion, chopped
1 cucumber, peeled and chopped
2 fresh tomatoes, diced
1 cup fresh mushrooms, sliced
1/4 cup green olives, sliced
1/4 cup black olives, sliced
1/2 lb. fresh spinach, washed and torn
1 tsp. dried basil

Cook pasta then run under cold water and drain. Set aside.

Make marinade by mixing sugar, vinegar, soup, oil and salt and pepper. Stir well with a fork, set aside.

In a extra large bowl, toss pasta and vegetables. Pour on marinade, and mix. Serve immediately or refrigerate until needed. Serves 6 generously.

My sister, Myra, took this recipe from my Aunt Carol and changed it a little to make a healthy, hearty, super satisfying salad. It satisfies mind, body and tastebuds. MBG

GREEK PASTA SALAD

1 lb. pasta (rotini, shells, or spaghetti)
3 roma tomatoes, diced
1 cup chopped carrots
1 cup chopped broccoli
1/2 cup sliced black olives
1/2 cup chopped onion
1/2 cup chopped red or green bell pepper
3/4 cup crumbled feta cheese
1 cup Greek Salad Dressing

Cook pasta according to package directions.
Drain and cool. In a large bowl, toss all ingredients.
Chill. Serves 8 - 10

GREEK SALAD DRESSING

1/2 cup olive oil
1/2 cup red wine vinegar
1 tsp. dried basil
1/2 tsp. dried oregano
2 cloves garlic, minced
1 Tbs. sugar
1 Tbs. lemon juice

Mix all ingredients and store in a jar in the fridge.
Shake well before using.

BLACK BEAN SALAD

4 cups cooked black beans
    (or 2 16-oz. cans)
1 1/2 cups frozen corn
1 cup frozen green peas
1/2 cup red bell pepper, chopped
1/2 cup green bell pepper, chopped
1/2 cup onion, chopped
1 can whole tomatoes, drained and chopped
1/4 cup lime juice
1/4 cup vegetable oil
1 Tbs. ground cumin
2 cloves garlic, minced
1/2 tsp. cayenne pepper
1/2 tsp. black pepper
1/2 tsp. salt

Combine beans, corn, peas, peppers, onion and tomatoes in a large bowl and toss. In a small bowl mix lime juice, oil, cumin, garlic, peppers and salt with a fork. Pour over salad and gently toss, refrigerate. Prepare at least two hours before serving. Makes 6-8 servings.

Another easy way to prepare this dish is to just add fresh homemade salsa to the black beans, corn and peas.

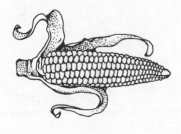

WALDORF SALAD

Make this salad in the fall when apples are fresh and ripe. It is good to use different types of apples to diversify the flavors of this salad. Try Rome, MacIntosh, Fiji, Brae-burn...There are a lot of apples in the world.

2 red apples
2 green apples
1/4 cup raisins
1/4 cup chopped walnuts
1/4 cup chopped celery
1 8 oz. can pineapple chunks
2/3 cup plain yogurt
1/4 cup mayonaisse

Cut apples into 1/2" chunks - leave the skins on. Toss them in a large bowl with the raisins, nuts, celery and drained pineapple. Save 3 Tbs. of the pineapple juice and mix with the yogurt and mayonnaise. Add to the fruit, toss and serve. Enough for 6 servings.

SIDE DISHES

Don't underestimate the power
of a side dish. It can turn an average
meal into something special.

MIMMY'S LIMA BEAN CASSEROLE

2-3 cups frozen lima beans, cooked and drained,
       reserving liquid
1/3 cup minced pimento
1/2 tsp. salt
1 cup grated Colby cheese
2 Tbs. ketchup
1 3/4 cup white sauce
2 Tbs. melted butter
1 cup plain breadcrumbs

Mix first six ingredients together in a casserole dish. Mix butter and breadcrumbs and place on top. Bake at 350° for 30 minutes.

WHITE SAUCE

3 Tbs. butter or margarine
3 Tbs. flour
1/2 tsp. salt
1/4 tsp. black pepper
1 1/2 cups milk (may use part liquid from
       lima beans)

Melt butter in a saucepan over low heat. Stir in flour, salt and pepper. Cook, stirring, until smooth and bubbly. Pour in milk. Heat to boiling, stirring constantly, then cook one minute until thickened.

This was a favorite dish at my family gatherings. My grandmother, Agnes Little, loved cooking for all her family. LKL

SPINACH SAUTE

The bright green color of this side dish makes a beautiful plate presentation.

 1 lb. fresh spinach, washed
 3 cloves garlic, chopped
 1 Tbs. butter or olive oil

Pick through spinach and remove stems. In a large skillet, melt oil or butter then add garlic. Sauté for one minute then add spinach. Cook until spinach is wilted and serve immediately. Serves 4.

CHRIS LEON

MEXICAN RICE CASSEROLE

1/2 medium onion, chopped
2 cloves garlic, minced
1/2 green bell pepper, chopped
1 Tbs. olive oil
1 10 oz. can Ro-Tel* tomatoes and chilies
1 cup rice
2 cups water (including liquid from tomatoes)
1 Tbs. chopped fresh parsley
1 tsp. cumin
1/2 cup grated Cheddar or Monterey Jack cheese
1/2 tsp. salt

Sauté onion, garlic and pepper in oil until tender. Pour veggies into a 2 1/2 quart casserole and add remaining ingredients, stir. Cover with lid or aluminum foil and bake at 350° for 55 minutes, or until liquid has been absorbed. Enjoy as a side dish for any meal. Stir before serving. Serves 6.

*Ro-Tel is a brand name of canned tomatoes and chilies. You will find them at your local grocery. Some stores have their own brand.

RICE PILAF

3 1/2 cups water
1 1/2 cups rice
1 Tbs. butter
2 bay leaves
1 tsp. saffron or dried chrysanthemum leaves

Combine water (1/3 of the mixture can be chicken broth), bay leaves and saffron and bring to a boil.

Melt butter in a saucepan, add rice and sauté, about 2 minutes. Add rice to boiling water, cover and reduce heat and simmer 25 - 30 minutes or until liquid is absorbed.

Guest Chef George Mikedes prepared this as a side dish to Chicken Byzantine. What an exquisite meal!

John Crider

GREEK GREEN BEANS

1 onion, chopped
3 cloves garlic, minced
1 Tbs. olive oil
2 Tbs. fresh parsley, chopped
1 28 oz. can peeled tomatoes, chopped, with juice
2 lbs. fresh green beans, steamed or
   2 lbs. frozen green beans
1 tsp. dried basil
1 tsp. dried oregano
1/4 tsp. salt
1/4 tsp. black pepper

In a large saucepan, sauté onion and garlic in oil for 4 minutes or until tender. Add parsley and tomatoes, cook another 3 minutes and add green beans, herbs, salt and pepper. Cook, stirring occasionally, until beans are done. Serve this with rice and Spanakopita, or any Greek dish. Serves 4–6.

DILLED GREEN BEANS

2 pounds fresh green beans, picked
1 bunch green onions, chopped,
2 cloves garlic, minced
1 Tbs. olive oil
2 Tbs. white wine
2 Tbs. fresh lemon juice
1/2 tsp. dried dill weed
Salt and pepper to taste

Steam beans in a large pot or place them in a micro-wave proof bowl, cover them with plastic, and cook on high for 3 – 5 minutes or until beans are tender.

In a large saucepan, sauté onions and garlic in oil until tender. Add wine, lemon juice and dill. Then add beans, toss and season. This side dish goes with just about anything, but seems to accompany fish and rice especially well. Serves 6.

Natural Foods Cafe
homemade soups
and sandwiches

INDIAN POTATOES AND PEAS

2 pounds small red potatoes
1 Tbs. butter or oil
1 Tbs. chopped garlic
1 Tbs. chopped onion
1 Tbs. fresh grated ginger
2-3 Tbs. fresh cilantro
2 tsp. whole cumin seed (not ground)
1 tsp. turmeric
1 10 ounce package frozen peas
salt and pepper to taste

Steam potatoes, leaving skins on, cool and cut into wedges.

Melt butter or oil in a large fry pan and sauté garlic and onion. Add potatoes and spices, mix well and continue to sauté. Stir in peas and serve with Curried Chicken or any Indian meal. Serves 4.

ROSEMARY POTATOES

8 small to medium red potatoes
4 Tbs. olive oil
4 cloves garlic, minced
1 Tbs. dried rosemary, crumbled
Salt and pepper to taste

Cut potatoes into 1-inch wedges. Lay them on a baking sheet and toss with oil, garlic, rosemary, salt and pepper. Bake at 350° for one hour or until baked through. Toss potatoes occasionally, so they won't stick to the pan. Serves 4 - 6.

BREADED CAULIFLOWER

1 large head cauliflower
4 Tbs. butter or margarine
3/4 cup cracker crumbs
1/2 tsp. seasoned salt

Break up the cauliflower into bite-sized pieces and steam until just tender – don't over cook. In the meantime, melt butter in a skillet and add crumbs. Sauté until crumbs are golden – be careful not to burn them. Toss crumbs with hot cauliflower in a bowl and serve. Serves 4.

This is an old-time favorite of my family. I think my mother made it to get us to eat our vegetables – it worked. MBG

CARDAMOM CARROTS

1 pound carrots
1 Tbs. butter
1 clove garlic, minced
1 Tbs. grated orange zest
1/8 tsp. ground cardamom
2 Tbs. orange juice

Peel carrots and cut into matchsticks.
In a skillet, sauté garlic in butter for two minutes. Add carrots, zest, cardamom and juice. Simmer until carrots are just tender and serve. Serves 4.

Cardamom is a spice that grows from pod bearing plants in the tropical forests of India. It is a seldom used spice with an incredible fragrance and unforgettable taste. For the best flavor in all your recipes, buy green pods and remove the seeds. Crush seeds with a mortar and pestle or a coffee grinder. (My mom wraps the pods in foil and smashes them with a hammer.)

MEDITERRANEAN COUSCOUS

2 Tbs. butter
1 bunch green onions, chopped
2 cloves garlic, minced
1/4 cup chopped parsley
2 cups vegetable broth
1 1/2 Tbs. sundried tomatoes, chopped in bits
2 cups couscous
1/2 cup pecans, chopped and toasted

In a saucepan, sauté onions and garlic in butter until tender. Add parsley, broth and tomatoes. Bring to a boil and add couscous. Remove from heat. Stir and cover and let sit for five minutes. Stir in pecans and serve immediately. Serves 4 - 6.

STEWED APPLES

4 large, firm apples*
1 tsp. ground cinnamon
1 Tbs. butter
2 Tbs. water
1/2 Tbs. brown sugar
Dash of cayenne pepper

Peel and core apples and cut into chunks. Place all ingredients in a thick-bottomed saucepan and cook, covered, over medium heat, stirring occasionally. Apples are done when tender (about 20 minutes). If you like them softer, cook them longer.

* It is best to use a tart cooking apple for this dish. We prefer Granny Smith, Braeburn, MacIntosh, or Rome. Use a combination if you like.

APPLE MANGO CHUTNEY

Chutney is an excellent condiment. Serve it with curried vegetables or as a topping for baked sweet potatoes.

 2 cups tart apples, peeled and chopped
 1 cup fresh mango, peeled and chopped
 1 lemon, peeled, chopped and seeded
 1/4 cup chopped onion
 1/2 cup raisins
 1/3 cup fresh ginger, peeled and chopped
 1/4 tsp. cinnamon
 1 cup cider vinegar
 3/4 cup brown sugar
 2 cloves garlic, minced
 1/4 tsp. cayenne pepper

Mix all ingredients in a large heavy-bottomed saucepan. Simmer on low for an hour or until fruit is soft. Store in the fridge for up to two weeks. Makes 2 1/2 cups.

YOGURT CHUTNEY SAUCE

 2 cups plain yogurt
 3 Tbs. apple mango chutney
 1 tsp. curry powder
 2 Tbs. dry white wine

Mix all ingredients in a food processor until smooth. Add to curried vegetables or store in fridge and use as a dipping sauce.

BREADS

Of all the things we make at the cafe, the smell of fresh baked bread is probably one of the most loved smells that comes out of our kitchen.

POPPY SEED MUFFINS

1 3/4 cup all-purpose flour
3/4 tsp. salt
1/4 cup sugar
2 tsp. baking powder
2 eggs
2 Tbs. oil or applesauce*
3/4 cup milk
1/4 cup poppy seeds
Grated lemon rind
1 Tbs. lemon juice

Mix together dry ingredients, then add wet ingredients. Fold until just blended, don't overmix, and pour into muffin tins. Bake at 400° for 20 - 25 minutes. Makes two dozen muffins.

*Using applesauce instead of oil makes these muffins lower in fat.

BLUEBERRY MUFFINS

Dry:
- 1 cup unbleached white flour
- 1 cup whole wheat pastry flour
- 4 tsp. baking powder
- 1/2 tsp. salt

Wet:
- 3 Tbs. honey
- 3/4 cup milk
- 1 egg, beaten
- 1/4 cup melted margarine

- 1 cup fresh blueberries

Blend dry ingredients. In separate bowl, stir wet ingredients. Pour liquid ingredients into dry ingredients, stir until just moistened. Add berries and stir until just mixed. Pour into greased muffin tins 2/3 full. Crumble topping on top of muffins (recipe below) if desired. Bake at 350° for 20 minutes.

Crumb Topping for Blueberry Muffins

- 1/2 cup margarine, softened
- 1/2 cup brown sugar
- 1/2 cup flour
- 1/2 cup rolled oats

Mix in bowl with a fork until crumbly.

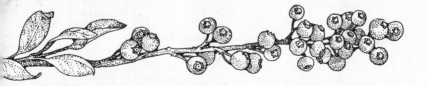

SCALLION BUTTERMILK BISCUITS

This easy recipe is from our friend, Rhonda Turman.

1 1/4 cup all-purpose flour
1/4 cup yellow cornmeal
2 tsp. baking powder
2 tsp. sugar
1/2 tsp. salt
1 1/2 Tbs. butter
4 medium scallions, finely chopped
1 cup buttermilk

In a large bowl, combine flour, cornmeal, baking powder, sugar and salt. Using fingertips, work in butter until blended. Add scallions, then stir in the buttermilk just until mixture comes together. Spoon dough onto the baking sheet in six equal mounds, about 2 inches apart. Bake 25 minutes at 350° until golden. Serve warm.

BUTTERMILK WAFFLES

To make breakfast extra special - add blueberries, apple chunks, sliced bananas or strawberries to your waffles. M'mmm.

1 1/4 cup all-purpose flour
3/4 cup whole wheat flour
2 Tbs. sugar
1 Tbs. baking powder
1/2 tsp. salt
3 large eggs, lightly beaten
6 Tbs. melted butter
1 1/2 cups buttermilk
1/2 tsp. vanilla

Stir the flour, sugar, powder and salt in a small mixing bowl. Beat the remaining ingredients in a large bowl. Gradually add the dry ingredients to the liquid – stirring until smooth. Pour 1/4 cup batter into hot waffle iron and bake until golden. Serve with butter and maple syrup.

ANISE SEED BREAD

Mary Ann Yarsinske baked this bread for the first skiers when the cafe was started in 1982. It is still as popular today as it was back then.

4 cups all-purpose flour
1 tsp. allspice
1 tsp. cinnamon
1 tsp. ground ginger
1/2 tsp. cloves
Dash of salt
2 1/2 tsp. baking powder
1 1/4 cup water
1 Tbs. anise seed
1 cup brown sugar
1 cup molasses
1/2 tsp. baking soda

In a large bowl, combine flour, spices, salt and baking powder. Set aside.

In a saucepan, simmer water and anise seed. Add sugar and molasses. When sugar is dissolved, remove from heat and add baking soda. Add wet mixture into the flour, stirring until smooth. Pour into two greased loaf pans and bake at 350° for 1 hour.

WHITE GRASS SKI TOURING CENTER

BANANA NUT ROUND

1 cup margarine or butter
2 cups sugar
4 eggs, beaten
2 cups all-purpose flour
2 cups whole wheat flour
2 tsp. baking soda
1 tsp. cinnamon
Pinch of salt
5 Tbs. sour cream
4 ripe bananas, smashed well
2 cups chopped walnuts

Cream butter and sugar, add beaten eggs. Mix well. Add flours sifted with soda, cinnamon and salt. Then add sour cream, beat well. Blend in bananas and nuts. Pour into a greased tube pan and bake at 350° for 1 hour and 20 minutes, or until inserted knife comes out clean. This recipe also fills two bread pans.

One day while cooking at The Mountain Institute on Spruce Knob, I found myself with an abundance of over ripe bananas and no bread pans. So I made a double bread recipe and poured it into a tube pan. It turned out delicious – and you can get 20 slices from this cake. That comes in handy when feeding a crowd.
MBG

PUMPKIN BREAD

2/3 cup vegetable oil
2 2/3 cup sugar
4 eggs
1 16 oz. can pumpkin
2/3 cup water
2 cups white flour
1 1/3 cup whole wheat pastry flour
2 tsp. baking soda
1 1/2 tsp. salt
1/2 tsp. baking powder
2 tsp. cinnamon
2 tsp. allspice
1/2 tsp. ground ginger
2/3 cup chopped nuts (optional)
2/3 cup raisins (optional)

Preheat oven to 350°. Cream oil, sugar, eggs, pumpkin and water in a large bowl. Blend in flours, soda, salt, powder and spices. Stir well. Pour into two 9 x 5 x 3 greased and floured loaf pans and bake 70 minutes or until inserted knife comes out clean. Cool slightly and remove from pan. Continue to cool on wire rack.

HOT SPICED CIDER

1 quart apple cider
1 - 2 tsp. cider spices (cinnamon, nutmeg, cloves, etc.)

Place spices in a tea ball and mull cider over low heat. Serve in mugs. It's a great accompaniment to pumpkin bread or oatmeal cookies. Frontier Herbs (see page 190) sells an excellent "Cider Mate" mix.

CORN BREAD

1 cup buttermilk
1 egg
2 Tbs. honey
2 tsp. baking powder
1/2 tsp. baking soda
1/2 tsp. salt
1 cup yellow cornmeal
1 cup all-purpose flour
3 Tbs. melted butter

Blend buttermilk, honey and egg. Then add powder, soda, salt, cornmeal and flour. Mix well and pour in melted butter, stir. Pour into a greased 9-inch round pie pan and bake at 400° for 15 - 20 minutes.

Hint: If you don't have buttermilk, you can make it by adding 1 tsp. white vinegar to 1 cup milk. Or, you can substitute yogurt for the buttermilk in this recipe.

White Grass Cafe

PIZZA DOUGH

1 pkg. dry yeast
1 Tbs. sugar
1 cup very warm beer (80° - 90°)
1/2 tsp. salt
1/2 tsp. black pepper
1 cup whole wheat flour
2 cups all-purpose flour

Place sugar and yeast in a mixing bowl – add warm beer (set the opened beer bottle or can in very hot water to warm it up.) Stir until yeast dissolves. Let it set 5 minutes. Then add salt, pepper and flour, a cup at a time, and mix well. Work the flour into the dough and knead for 10 minutes, or until dough is soft. Let it rise 1 - 1 & 1/2 hours, or until doubled in size, then press in a greased pan. Load up with your favorite toppings and bake at 450° for 20 minutes or until crust is brown.

Some of our favorite pizza toppings:

Marinara sauce (see page 94)   lots of garlic
pesto (see page 106)   sliced mushrooms
sliced fresh tomatoes   thinly sliced onions
herbed feta cheese   grated carrots
fresh spinach   grated Mozzarella
sliced artichoke hearts   fresh basil leaves

WHOLE WHEAT PASKA

1 cup milk
1/2 cup butter or margarine
2/3 cup sugar
1 tsp. salt
1 1/2 Tbs. dry yeast
1 tsp. sugar
1/4 cup warm water
2 eggs, beaten
2 tsp. vanilla
2 cups whole wheat flour
2 1/2 cups all-purpose flour

Scald milk, then add butter to the saucepan. Add 2/3 cup of sugar and salt. Cool slightly.

In a large bowl, dissolve yeast in 1 tsp. sugar and warm warm water, let sit 5 minutes. Add eggs, vanilla and 2 cups of the flour and lukewarm milk mixture and beat with a wooden spoon. Add the rest of the flour and beat well.

Knead (this will be a sticky dough) for 5-10 minutes. Place dough in a large greased bowl and let rise until doubled. Gently deflate and let rise again. Put in two 8 1/2" loaf pans and bake at 325° for 30 - 45 minutes.

This recipe is from my Aunt Olga's mother, Mary Kondratik. It is a traditional Eastern European bread made at Easter. A sweet and hearty bread, Paska makes great toast. MBG

ITALIAN BREAD

4 - 6 cups all-purpose flour
1 Tbs. sugar
1 Tbs. salt
2 Tbs. baking yeast
1 Tbs. soft margarine or butter
1 3/4 cup very warm water (120° to 130°)
Cornmeal for dusting
2 Tbs. vegetable oil
1 egg white + 1 Tbs. cold water, mixed

In a large bowl, mix 3 cups flour, sugar, salt and yeast. Add margarine. Gradually add water and beat, with a mixer, for 2 minutes at medium speed. Add 3/4 cup flour, and mix, with your hands, again. Stir in enough flour to make a stiff dough. Knead 8 - 10 minutes until smooth.

Cover, and let rest for 20 minutes. Form into two loaves. Place on a greased and cornmealed cookie sheet. Brush with oil and cover. Refrigerate 2 to 24 hours. Before baking, let sit at room temp. for 10 minutes and make 3 or 4 slits with a knife. Bake at 425° for 20 minutes, brush with egg wash, and return to oven for 5 - 10 minutes longer or until golden brown. Makes 2 loaves.

This recipe is from Mary Ann Yarsinske
one of our favorite people.

SWEDISH CARDAMOM BREAD

2 pkgs. dry yeast (2 Tbs.)
2 cups scalded milk, cooled
1/4 cup warm water
3/4 cup sugar
2 eggs, beaten
2 tsp. crushed cardamom
1 tsp. salt
1 stick melted butter
8-10 cups all-purpose flour
1 egg beaten with 1 Tbs. water
1/2 cup sliced almonds

In a large mixing bowl, dissolve yeast in the warm water. Stir in milk, sugar, eggs, cardamom and salt. Stir in 5 cups flour and mix well. Then add melted butter, stir until blended. Add 3-4 cups more flour, mixing to a stiff dough. Turn out on a board and knead until smooth and satiny.

Place in greased bowl, cover and let rise until doubled in bulk (about 1 hour). Punch down and allow to rise again for 45 minutes.

Divide dough into three equal parts. Then divide each piece into thirds and make long logs. Braid the dough and place on a greased sheet. Let rise 20 minutes. Brush top with beaten egg and sprinkle with sliced almonds. Bake at 375° for 25 - 30 minutes. Makes three loaves.

This very special bread is made by my mother every Christmas and Easter. It is probably the tastiest bread I've ever eaten. My Aunt Martha will forego the entire meal and eat only bread and butter. MBG

SUNFLOWER OATMEAL BREAD

1 pkg. yeast (1 Tbs.)
1/2 tsp. sugar
1 1/4 cups warm water
1 1/4 cups warm buttermilk
1/4 cup honey
2 Tbs. molasses
2 Tbs. butter
1 cup whole wheat flour
4-5 cups all-purpose flour
1 cup rolled oats
3/4 cup sunflower seeds
1 Tbs. millet
1 Tbs. salt
1 egg, lightly beaten
Egg glaze (1 egg beaten with 1 tsp. water)

In a small bowl, combine yeast, sugar and warm water. Stir to dissolve and let stand 5 minutes.

Combine buttermilk, honey, molasses and butter in a small bowl.

In a large bowl, combine wheat flour, oats, sunflower seeds, millet and salt. Add buttermilk mixture, yeast and egg. Whisk hard for about 3 minutes and add all-purpose flour, 1/2 cup at a time, beating until mixed well. Knead until a soft dough is formed.

Cover and let rise until doubled (about 1 1/2 hours). Punch down, divide into three round loaves, cover with plastic and let rise 30 minutes. Brush with egg glaze and sprinkle with oats. Bake at 375° for 40 minutes.

This is a slight variation of a fabulous bread made by Anne Weatherford, a former cafe baker. She is now the pastry chef in New Orleans.

WHOLE WHEAT BREAD
White Grass Dinner Bread

Sponge:
      1 Tbs.+ 2 tsp. baking yeast
      1 1/2 cups wrist warm water
      A drop of honey
      1 cup whole wheat flour
      1 cup white flour

Mix:
      4 Tbs. melted butter
      1/3 cup honey
      2 tsp. salt

Add yeast to water, add sweetener. Stir, let stand 5 minutes. Beat in flour then cover with a towel. Let rise 45 minutes in a warm place. Prepare mix and add to sponge once it has foamed up.

    Add in 1/2 cup at a time:
      2 cups whole wheat flour
      2 cups white flour

Knead well and let rise, covered, until double in size. Punch down, divide in half and form loaves. Place in greased loaf pans to rise (covered). Bake at 375° for 30-40 minutes. Turn out of pan to a cooling rack. We bet you can't wait till it's cool to taste it! Makes 2 loaves.

ICE BOX ROLLS

2 Tbs. margarine
1/2 cup sugar
2 tsp. salt
2 cups hot water
2 eggs, beaten
1 Tbs. baking yeast
1/4 cup warm water
8 - 9 cups all-purpose flour
2 Tbs. melted butter

Pour hot water over margarine, sugar and salt. Stir until it dissolves. Let sit until lukewarm.

Dissolve yeast in warm water and add, with eggs, to the first mixture. Mix in enough flour and knead to make a soft dough. Cover with plastic wrap and store in fridge until needed. When ready to bake, pinch off rolls, and let rise in a warm place until doubled. Rub tops with melted butter and bake at 375° for 15 - 20 minutes.

MY OWN FAVORITE COFFEE RING

A beautiful recipe from Laurie's Grandmother.

 1/2 recipe of Ice Box Rolls (see page 90)
 2 Tbs. butter
 1/4 cup brown sugar
 1/4 cup chopped nuts (pecans or walnuts)
 1 tsp. cinnamon
 2 Tbs. chopped raisins
 1 Tbs. melted butter

Roll Ice Box dough to about 1/2" thick in a rectangle shape. Dot liberally with butter. Spread with brown sugar, nuts, cinnamon and raisins. Roll as you would a jelly roll. Put on a greased baking sheet and pinch ends together to form a ring. Rub with melted butter. Cut, leaving the layer of dough at the center uncut. Turn each piece with the cut side up. Let rise and bake at 375° for 15 min.

Cut dough
on dotted
lines and
twist each
roll on
its side.

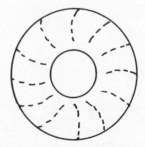

More Love Letters

"Dear Mary Beth and Laurie,
      Just a note to tell you how much I love your cook-
book. I use it more than any other (and I have a con-
siderable number of them). Every time I try a new recipe
I letter grade it and there are a remarkable number of A's
and a few A+'s. You're right - I'll never buy salsa from a
jar again.
      Bonnie's Ceylonese Chicken was a special hit with
'Easty'...and now we are both blaming Bonnie, Ron,
and Mary Beth for our Indonesian cravings! Thanks
again for making food from my kitchen interesting
and delectable!"

>   Best Wishes,
>   Ajax Eastman

"...My friends who recently packed their bags to spend
two years high in the Hindu-Kush Karakorum range in
Pakistan, took only two cookbooks with them. Your wonderful White Grass Cafe Cookbook was one of them.
Thanks for the good eats!

>   Jason Espie
>   Harrisonburg, VA

"...I am in love with the cookbook. We live a half hour
from the nearest grocery store which sometimes means
we make up some of the most god-awful concoctions
to avoid a trip. Your cookbook is full of great recipes
from things which are lurking in the pantry. Bravo
Laurie and Mary Beth!"

>   Mar Startari
>   Butler, TN

VEGETARIAN ENTREES

Our cafe began as a vegetarian restaurant and people still seek us out for this reason. We have expanded our menu to include fish, seafood and chicken, but our most popular entrees are meatless.

MARINARA SAUCE

2 Tbs. olive oil
1 large onion, diced
4 cloves garlic, minced
1/2 cup fresh parsley, chopped
2 28 oz. cans chopped tomatoes
2 28 oz. cans tomato puree
1/2 cup dry red wine
1 Tbs. dried basil
1 Tbs. dried oregano
1 tsp. salt
1 tsp. sugar
1 tsp. black pepper

In a large saucepan, sauté onion and garlic in oil until tender, (about 5 minutes). Add parsley, tomatoes and puree. Stir in wine and seasonings and let sauce simmer at least 30 minutes. The longer this sauce can cook, the better it tastes. Just make sure you stir it occasionally to keep from sticking.

This is a basic marinara sauce. To jazz it up, try adding grated carrots, squash, zucchini, chopped green or red peppers, or any other favorite vegetable.

> Most of the recipes in this book call for using dried herbs, because, they are readily available year-round. If you have access to fresh herbs, by all means, use them. Remember to double the amount listed for dried herbs.

EGGPLANT PARMESAN

This is a non-traditional way to make this dish, but it is lower in fat and even tastier than breading and frying the eggplant. Serve this dish with salad, crusty bread and hot pasta on the side. Your family will love it.

2 large or 3 medium eggplants
2 tsp. salt
2 Tbs. olive oil
2 cloves garlic, minced
2 cups Marinara sauce, see page 94
1/4 cup Parmesan cheese
1/2 cup grated Mozzarella cheese

Peel eggplants and slice into 1/2-inch slices. In a large bowl, pour in one quart of water and salt, stir. Place eggplant in water and let soak for about 20 - 30 minutes. This will take any bitterness out of the eggplant. Drain.

In a small saucepan, sauté garlic in oil for 2 minutes. Brush eggplant with oil and garlic and place on a cookie sheet. Bake at 400° in a pre-heated oven for about 20 minutes, until eggplant is tender. Place eggplant in a casserole dish, pour on Marinara, sprinkle with both cheeses. Bake for 30 minutes, uncovered, at 350°, or until cheese has lightly browned. Serves 4.

ITALIAN STIR FRY

This is quite a meal in itself. All you need is salad, bread and four hearty appetites.

1 Tbs. olive oil
1 onion, sliced and quartered
3 cloves garlic, minced
1 yellow squash, sliced and quartered
1 red bell pepper, sliced thin
1 green bell pepper, sliced thin
8 oz. fresh mushrooms, sliced thin
1 pound penne or rotini pasta
3 cups Marinara sauce, see page 94
Parmesan cheese for garnish

In a large skillet, heat oil and sauté onion and garlic. Cook for two minutes then add squash, cook for 2 more minutes. Add peppers and cook another few minutes. Mushrooms go in next - cook 3 minutes longer or until all veggies are cooked but not mushy.

Cook pasta according to package directions, drain. Portion pasta into large flat bowls. Cover with a ladle of hot Marinara sauce and add a heap of vegetables. Serve immediately with Parmesan. Serves 4.

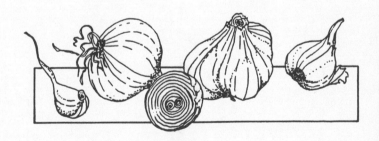

EASIEST EVER SPINACH LASAGNA

In this recipe, you don't cook the noodles, they steam as the lasagna bakes. For a cafe favorite, serve as a hefty 4-inch square with salad and homemade bread.

1 10 oz pkg. frozen chopped spinach, thawed
2 15 oz. ricotta or cottage cheese
1 tsp. dried basil
1 tsp. minced garlic
1/4 cup Parmesan cheese
3 eggs
Salt and pepper to taste
1 quart Marinara sauce, (see page 94)
1 box lasagna noodles (uncooked)
1 1/2 cups grated mozzarella
1/3 cup water

Squeeze water out of spinach and mix with ricotta, eggs, basil, garlic, Parmesan, and salt and pepper. In a 9" x 13" baking pan, pour in 1/2 cup sauce to cover the bottom .

Line pan with uncooked noodles, then spoon half of the filling and spread evenly over the noodles. Sprinkle 1/2 cup mozzarella. Then a layer of sauce and again noodles, filling, cheese and sauce. Top with remaining mozzarella. Drizzle water over the top, cover with foil and bake at 350° for 45 minutes. Remove cover and bake an additional 10 - 15 minutes to brown the top. Take out of the oven and let sit about 15 minutes before serving. Serves 6-10.

"MEATLESS" BALLS

Our friend, Bobbie Moore, gave us this recipe. They are excellent served with the barbecue sauce (below) as an appetizer, or with your favorite Italian dish in place of real meatballs.

1 lb. firm tofu, crumbled
1/2 cup bread crumbs
1 medium onion, chopped fine
1/2 cup chopped walnuts
3 cloves garlic, chopped
2 tsp. dried basil
1 egg

2 tsp. dried oregano
1/2 tsp. dried thyme
1 tsp. black pepper
1/4 cup soy sauce
1 Tbs. chopped,
    fresh parsley

Mix together all ingredients, using your hands. If too wet, add more breadcrumbs - if too dry, add a little water. Roll into balls and place on an oiled baking sheet. Bake at 350° for 10 minutes. Turn each ball over and bake an additional 10 - 15 minutes. Serve with barbecue sauce or any other dipping sauce.

BARBECUE SAUCE

1/4 cup chopped onion
2 cloves garlic, minced
2 Tbs. brown sugar
1/4 tsp. cayenne
1/4 cup lemon juice
1/2 Tbs. dried mustard

1 cup ketchup
1/2 cup water
1/2 tsp. salt
2 Tbs. vinegar
3 Tbs. Worchestershire
1/2 tsp. celery seed

Sauté garlic and onion in 1 tsp. oil in a saucepan. Add remaining ingredients and bring to a slow boil. Simmer over low heat for 20 minutes. It's ready to serve or store in the refrigerator for future use. Use this sauce on grilled tofu or chicken. Mmmm.

LINGUINI WITH ASPARAGUS, GARLIC AND LEMON

1/2 cup onion, chopped
2 cloves garlic, minced
1 Tbs. olive oil
1 Tbs. butter
1/2 pound fresh asparagus
2 Tbs. dry white wine
1/2 tsp. dried basil
1 Tbs. lemon juice
2 Tbs. Parmesan cheese
1/3 pound linguini

In a skillet, sauté onion and garlic in olive oil and butter until golden. Slice asparagus diagonally 1/4" thick and add to the skillet. Cook 2 minutes then add wine, basil and lemon juice, then add 1 Tbs. water. Cook linguini according to package directions, drain. Toss with asparagus, sprinkle with Parmesan and enjoy. Serves 2.

RATATOUILLE

Ratatouille is a hearty vegetable stew that can be made a number of ways. This is a very delicious and easy version. The key is to use fresh ingredients. If you have fresh herbs, use them – double the amount of dried herbs.

1 large eggplant, peeled and cut into 1/2" cubes
3 Tbs. olive oil
1 large onion, chopped
4 cloves garlic, minced
1 red bell pepper, chopped
1 green bell pepper, chopped
1 large zucchini, sliced
1 yellow squash, sliced
8 ripe plum tomatoes, chopped
   or a 28 oz. can diced tomatoes
1 small can tomato paste
1/3 cup water
1 tsp. black pepper
1/2 tsp. dried thyme
1 1/2 tsp. dried basil
1 tsp. dried oregano

Soak cubed eggplant in salted water for 30 minutes, drain. Heat oil in a large Dutch oven and sauté eggplant over medium-high heat for 5 minutes. Reduce heat and add onions, garlic, peppers, zucchini and squash. Stir and cook 5 minutes. Add tomatoes, paste, water, pepper and herbs. Stir well. Cover and simmer on low heat for 45 minutes, stirring occasionally. If it is too thick, add some water, a tablespoon at a time to thin it to your taste. If too soupy, let it simmer, uncovered to cook away some liquid. Hot brown rice or baked polenta complement this well. Serves 6.

SPANAKOPITA

1 Tbs. butter
2 medium onions, chopped
1 1/2 cups ricotta or cottage cheese
2 cups crumbled feta cheese
2 10-oz. pkgs. frozen chopped spinach,
       thawed and water squeezed out
6 eggs
1 tsp. dried basil
1 tsp. dried dill weed
1 tsp. dried oregano
1/2 tsp. salt
1/8 tsp. black pepper
1 lb. pkg. filo dough, thawed
1 cup (2 sticks) butter, melted

Sauté onions in 1 Tbs. butter until soft. In a large bowl, mix cottage cheese, feta, spinach, eggs, herbs, salt and pepper. Add onions and mix well.

Open filo and take out two sheets at a time, laying in a 9"x13" pan and brushing with butter, generously. Stack 8 sheets of filo, then spoon on half of the filling and spread over the pan. Continue to layer filo in "twos", being sure to brush them with butter. Place 4 sheets down, and spoon remainder of the filling. Pile the rest of the sheets on top and tuck in around the edges. Bake at 400° for 1 hour or until golden. Let this dish sit for at least 15 minutes before cutting.

> Don't be intimidated by working with filo dough! It's not as scary as the instructions of the box say. This is a fabulous and relatively easy dish.

VEGETARIAN MOUSSAKA

2 cups sliced eggplant
1/4 cup olive oil
Salt and pepper
2 Tbs. dried mint
2 cups sliced potatoes (1/8" thick)
1 1/4 cups sliced zucchini
1 1/4 cup sliced yellow squash
1 medium onion, chopped
1 Tbs. tomato paste
    or 1/4 cup dried tomatoes, rejuvenated
2 Tbs. dried basil
2 Tbs. fresh parsley
1/4 cup dry Vermouth or white wine (optional)

Peel eggplant, slice and soak in a bowl of cold salt water at least one hour to remove any bitterness. Pat dry and brush with olive oil and sprinkle with mint. Bake at 450°, 6 -7 minutes on each side, or until browned.

In a deep 9" x 12" pan, layer potatoes, then eggplant, then zucchini and squash.

In a saucepan, sauté onion in oil. Add tomato paste or tomatoes, basil, parsley and wine. Simmer 3 minutes and spread over vegetables. Bake at 350° for 20 minutes. Cool to room temperature. Make sauce (see page 103) and pour over vegetables. Bake at 350° for 30 - 40 minutes, or until top is slightly brown and bubbly. Cool for 30 minutes before cutting into 3 - 4 inch squares and serving.

George Mikedes wanted to cook at the cafe, so he accommodated us by making this traditional meat dish with only vegetables. It is delicious. The letter on the next page was received by a friend and fan of George's cooking.

CREMA SAUCE

1/2 cup butter
6 Tbs. flour
1 tsp. gr. nutmeg
4 eggs, beaten

4 cups hot milk, or
    1/2 milk & 1/2 cream
White pepper to taste
1 cup grated Romano

Melt butter in a heavy saucepan and gradually add flour, stirring constantly until flour browns. Add nutmeg and mix well. When roux is thick and bubbly, lower heat and slowly add milk, stirring constantly. Then add eggs and white pepper, blend. Add Romano and stir until sauce thickens. Sauce is ready, continue with directions on Moussaka recipe.

Dear Chip and Laurie,
   I know that you have been getting plenty of good reviews for the skiing part of your operation, but I thought that you deserved equal publicity for the marvelous food. I hope that this gets printed – and that you don't mind releasing the recipe. Reese thinks I should just have asked when we were there. Anyway...Please feel flattered –we had a great time.
                                        Pam

                          125 Greenwood Road
                          Staunton, VA 24401
                          February 26, 1996

GOURMET
560 Lexington Ave.
New York, NY 10022

Dear Editor:
   We had two amazingly delicious meals while skiing at the White Grass Ski Touring Center near Davis, West Virginia. The Vegetarian Moussaka was outstanding for its delicacy and we would love to have the recipe if you can possibly obtain it.
                          Pamela Patrick and Reese Bull

HALUSHKI
Noodles and Cabbage

1 small head cabbage
1 medium onion, chopped
6 Tbs. butter or margarine
1 12 oz. pkg. wide egg noodles
Salt and pepper to taste

Boil water to cook noodles according to package directions. In the meantime, grate cabbage (like for cole slaw.)

In a large skillet melt butter and saute onions and cabbage over med-low heat until tender. The cabbage will usually be done when the noodles are cooked. Drain noodles and toss with cabbage and onions. Serves 4.

Try it as a different accompaniment to a vegetable stir fry, instead of rice.

This is a Slovak dish from my grandmother.
She made her own noodles from scratch.
The only thing better than this was her
Pierogies. It is Gwyer family comfort food.
MBG

HALUPKI
Vegetarian Stuffed Cabbage

1 cup dry bulgur
1 1/2 cups boiling water
1 large onion, minced
4 cloves garlic, minced
1 cup rice (cooked for 10 min., and drained)
1 red bell pepper, minced
1 green bell pepper, minced
1 medium yellow squash, grated
1 medium zucchini, grated
2 carrots, grated
1/2 cup chopped fresh parsley
2 - 3 loose heads cabbage
2 28 oz. cans diced tomatoes with juice
1 tsp. dried basil

In a small bowl, pour boiling water over bulgur and cover for 10 minutes, until it has swelled.

Sauté onion, garlic and bell peppers for 3 - 4 minutes. In a large bowl, mix bulgur, rice and all the vegetables except the cabbage.

The cabbage must be parboiled in a large pot of water to soften the leaves so they pull off the head easily. Take a cabbage leaf and place 1/3 cup of the filling along the bottom edge. Roll up, tucking the sides in and place in a large covered baking dish or dutch oven. After all the cabbage leaves have been rolled, pour tomatoes over the top and sprinkle with basil. Cover and bake at 275° for 2 1/2 - 3 hours.

> This is another recipe from my grandmother. She made them with ground chuck, but I prefer the more diverse taste of vegetables. It is a time consuming process, but worth it. MBG

SPINACH PESTO

3 - 4 cups fresh spinach, cleaned, stems removed
1 cup fresh parsley
4 cloves garlic
1/3 cup butter, melted
1 Tbs. olive oil
3/4 cup Parmesan cheese
2 tsp. dried basil
2 tsp. dried oregano
1/2 tsp. salt
1/2 tsp. pepper
1/2 cup walnuts

Blend all ingredients in a food processor until smooth. Stir into hot pasta. For a creamy pesto, add 4 Tbs. of pesto to the Fettuccini Alfrieda recipe on page 107. Pesto can be stored in the refrigerator for up to one week and can also be frozen.

It's not easy to find fresh basil in the mountains in the dead of winter, so we substituted fresh spinach for this recipe. It's delicious. If you have any fresh basil, by all means, add it to this recipe.

FETTUCCINI ALFRIEDA

This is an easy and lowfat version of a traditional favorite. (And it tastes even better.) The next time you want noodles, try this as an entrée or side dish.

1 cup boiling water
1 8 oz. pkg. nonfat or lowfat cream cheese, room temp.
1/3 cup Parmesan cheese
1/4 cup fresh parsley, chopped (optional)
1 pound fettuccini or linguini
2 cloves garlic, minced
1 Tbs. butter

In a bowl, mix boiling water and cream cheese until smooth – whisk with a fork. Add cheese and parsley.

In the meantime, cook pasta. While it is draining, sauté garlic and butter in the pasta pot. Return pasta to pot, toss, and pour in sauce. Toss well and serve. Serves 3 - 4 as an entrée, or 6 as a side dish.

Adding a little pesto to this dish makes a fabulous meal. See page 106 for our pesto recipe. If you are a seafood lover, you'll find on page 152 how to further accent this dish.

MIMMY'S MACARONI AND CHEESE

2 cups elbow macaroni
2 quarts water
1/2 tsp. salt
2 Tbs. margarine
1/4 lb. saltine crackers (one stack)
1 12 oz. pkg. colby cheese, grated
Salt and pepper to taste
4 cups milk

Cook macaroni in water and salt until al dente, drain. In a greased casserole dish, layer in this order: noodles, crushed crackers, dots of margarine, cheese and salt and pepper. Fill casserole with milk to top of macaroni. Cover and bake at 350° for 45 minutes, or until bubbly. To brown the top, bake uncovered for an additional 5 minutes.

JAPANESE VEGGIE CAKES
O Konomi Yaki

1 Tbs. vegetable oil
1 Tbs. sesame oil
1/2 medium cabbage, sliced very thin
1/4 cup chopped red bell pepper
4 cloves garlic, minced
6 green onions, chopped
2 carrots, grated
2 Tbs. fresh grated ginger root
1/2 pound fresh mushrooms, sliced
1/2 pound fresh spinach
3 Tbs. flour
3 eggs
2 Tbs. soy sauce
1/2 tsp. crushed red pepper flakes
1 Tbs. toasted sesame seeds

Heat oils in a wok. Cook veggies in this order, waiting 1 minute after each addition: cabbage, bell pepper, garlic, onions, carrots, ginger, mushrooms and spinach. Transfer to a bowl and cool.

Beat flour, eggs, soy sauce and red pepper flakes, blend with veggies. Spoon batter into a lightly oiled skillet, making three inch cakes, and sauté until golden. Sprinkle with sesame seeds. These can be kept warm in the oven until all cakes are ready to serve. Serve with Hot Oriental Dipping Sauce, see page 141.

White Grass Cafe

CURRIED VEGETABLES

A vegetarian delight, this is a fine accompaniment or entrée. Serve with rice, pita and a chutney or raita for a delicious Indian meal.

2 carrots, peeled and chopped
1 cup cauliflower pieces
1 cup broccoli pieces
2 Tbs. vegetable oil
1 medium onion, chopped
3 cloves garlic, minced
1 large potato, baked or boiled and cubed
1 large sweet potato, cooked and cubed
1 10 oz. pkg. frozen peas
1 Tbs. fresh ginger, grated
1 Tbs. curry powder
1 tsp. turmeric
1/4 tsp. salt
Dash of cayenne pepper

Lightly steam carrots, cauliflower and broccoli, set aside. In a large skillet or wok, heat oil over med-high heat. Add onion and garlic, cook for 3 minutes. Add carrots and cauliflower. Toss in remaining ingredients and mix gently. Simmer vegetables until all are cooked to your liking and serve. For extra flavor, mix in Yogurt Chutney Sauce, see page 74. Serves 4 as an entrée, 6 as a side dish.

> If you don't like one of these vegetables, substitute with green beans, chick peas, squash, zucchini, or green peppers. Any of these would make nice additions to this recipe.

PAD THAI
(THAI NOODLES)

1/2 pound dried rice noodles, (1/8" thick)
1/4 cup fish sauce
1/4 cup cider vinegar
1/4 cup sugar
2 Tbs. vegetable oil
4 cloves garlic, minced
1/2 pound firm tofu, cut into chunks
2 eggs, beaten
6 green onions, chopped
1/2 pound mung bean sprouts
2 Tbs. dried chiles, chopped
3/4 cup roasted peanuts, chopped
Lime wedges

Soak noodles in a large bowl of warm water 30 minutes to soften, drain.

In the meantime, make sauce by mixing fish sauce, vinegar and sugar.

In a wok, heat oil and sauté garlic. Add noodles and tofu, cook 2 minutes and pour in sauce. Cook until sauce bubbles; make room in the middle of the wok and add eggs – stir until cooked and toss with noodles. Gently fold in green onions, sprouts and chiles. Toss and cook 2 minutes. Place noodles on plates, sprinkle with chopped peanuts and serve with lime wedges. Enough for 4.

This is a vegetarian version of this Asian recipe. It is usually made with chicken, shrimp and/or pork. It's also nice to add chopped broccoli or fresh greens to this dish to add both color and nutrients.

LO MEIN

1/2 lb. linguini or spaghetti noodles
2 Tbs. oil
1/2 onion, chopped
3 cloves garlic, chopped
1 cup broccoli florets
1 cup cauliflower florets
2 carrots, sliced thin
1 red bell pepper, chopped
1 cup sliced fresh mushrooms
1 cup fresh spinach leaves, washed
1 cup fresh snow peas

In a large pot, boil water and cook noodles according to package directions. In the meantime, heat oil in a wok and sauté onion and garlic, stirring constantly, for one minute. Add broccoli, cauliflower, carrots, pepper, mushrooms, spinach and snow peas one at a time. Wait one minute to let them cook before adding the next vegetable. Pour 1 cup Sesame Garlic Sauce over veggies and cook for another minute. Toss noodles and veggies and serve hot. Serves 4.

SESAME GARLIC SAUCE

3/4 cup soy sauce
1/4 cup vegetable oil
1 Tbs. toasted sesame oil
3 Tbs. grated fresh ginger

2 cloves garlic, minced
Juice from 1/2 lemon
1 Tbs. sugar

Pour all ingredients into a jar and shake well. Use immediately or store in refrigerator.

SPINACH MUSHROOM ENCHILADAS

5 - 6 medium potatoes
1 Tbs. vegetable oil
2 medium onions, chopped
4 cloves garlic, chopped
12 oz. mushrooms, sliced
2 10 oz. pkg. frozen spinach
    or 1 lb. fresh spinach
1 Tbs. ground cumin
1 Tbs. seasoned salt
1 dozen large flour tortillas
1 cup grated Monterey Jack cheese
4 cups Garlic Bechamel Sauce*

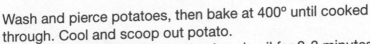

Wash and pierce potatoes, then bake at 400° until cooked through. Cool and scoop out potato.

In a skillet, sauté garlic and onions in oil for 2-3 minutes then add mushrooms. Sauté another 3 minutes. Squeeze excess water from frozen spinach and add to the skillet (or add fresh spinach) and cook until heated through. Mix potatoes and mushroom/spinach mixture in a large bowl. Add cumin and seasoned salt.

Put 1/4 cup of the filling on each flour tortilla, add a sprinkle of cheese and roll up. Place tortillas in a baking dish. Cover with Garlic Bechamel Sauce (*see page 157), bake at 350° for 20-30 minutes. Enjoy. Makes 6 servings.

The addition of potatoes to this dish was purely accidental. One busy Saturday night I accidentally dumped in too much seasoned salt and we had to add potatoes to diminish the salty taste (Ruth Melnick saved the day). We found that it actually tasted better with potatoes. And from that day on, our enchiladas always included potatoes. MBG

BEAN AND CHEESE ENCHILADAS

Serve these with fresh lettuce, sour cream, guacamole, salsa – all your Mexican favorites.

1 10 oz. can refried beans
1 Tbs. oil
1 medium onion, chopped
3 cloves garlic, minced
1 dozen corn tortillas
2 cups shredded Cheddar or Monterey Jack

Sauce:
2 Tbs. olive oil
1/2 cup chopped onion
2 cloves garlic, minced
1 Tbs. chili powder
1 cup tomato puree
1/2 cup vegetable broth
1 tsp. cumin
Salt and pepper to taste

In a saucepan, sauté onion and garlic in oil until tender. Add beans and cook, stirring occasionally, for 3 minutes.

In the meantime, make the sauce by cooking onion and garlic in oil until tender. Add chili powder, tomato puree, broth and spices, stir well. Take a tortilla and spread on a spoonful of beans, sauce and cheese. Roll and place in a baking dish, seam side down. After rolling all the tortillas, pour remaining sauce over the enchiladas and sprinkle with cheese. Cover and bake at 350° for 20 minutes. Serves 4-6.

BLACK BEAN CAKES

4 cups cooked black beans
3 cloves garlic
1 medium onion, diced
1 green bell pepper, diced
1 Tbs. vegetable oil
1 Tbs. ground cumin
1/2 tsp. black pepper
1/4 tsp. cayenne pepper
1 egg
1 Tbs. flour
3 Tbs. vegetable oil

Puree beans in a food processor or mash until soft. In a skillet, sauté garlic, onion and green pepper in oil until tender and cool slightly. Add to beans and mix in all spices then egg and flour, mix well. Form bean mixture into patties and sauté for 3 - 4 minutes on each side, they won't get too brown. Serve with fresh salsa (page 22) and Mexican white sauce (page 117).

Usually, we serve bean cakes as an entree with rice and cheese quesadillas. They can be made smaller and served as appetizers.

MEXICAN LASAGNA

1 can refried beans
8 oz. grated Monterey Jack cheese
1 pint sour cream
1 pint salsa
18 corn tortillas

In a 9 x 13" baking pan, spread 2 Tbs. salsa thinly over the bottom. Lay tortillas in pan and spread part of the beans then cheese, sour cream and salsa. Continue layers ending with tortillas and cheese. Bake at 350° for 30 minutes or until cheese starts to brown on top. Cut into squares and serve hot.

You can jazz up this recipe by adding extra layers of vegetables. Try some or all of these:

sliced avocados   fresh tomatoes
black beans   crumbled tofu
sautéed onions   chopped green pepper
sautéed squash   fresh or frozen corn
   or zucchini

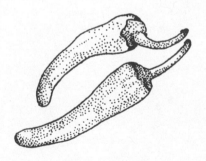

BLACK BEAN BURRITOS

1 Tbs. vegetable oil
3 cloves garlic, chopped
1 medium onion, chopped
1 green bell pepper, chopped
4 cups cooked black beans
3/4 cup chopped tomatoes, canned or fresh
2 tsp. ground cumin
1/2 tsp. cayenne pepper
1 pkg. large flour tortillas
2 cups shredded Cheddar cheese

Sauté garlic, onion and green pepper in oil for 4 minutes or until tender. In the meantime, heat beans in a saucepan, add onion mixture, tomatoes and spices, mix well. Spoon 1/4 cup of hot filling onto a flour tortilla, sprinkle with cheese and roll up. Place burritos on a baking sheet until all are rolled. Cover well with aluminum foil and place in a hot oven (400°) for 20 minutes. Place two burritos on a plate and spoon on a helping of red, white and green sauces (salsa, Mexican White Sauce (below) and guacamole. Serves 4 heartily with Mexican Rice Casserole (see page 64).

MEXICAN WHITE SAUCE

1 envelope ranch dressing mix
1 16 oz. container sour cream
1 Tbs. minced jalapeno pepper
1/2 tsp. ground cumin
1/4 tsp. black pepper
1 Tbs. minced garlic

Combine all ingredients and mix very well. Refrigerate and serve with burritos or any favorite Mexican dish.

WEST VIRGINIA CORN PONE

1 medium onion, chopped
3 cloves garlic, chopped
1 Tbs. vegetable oil
2 cups cooked pinto beans
1 can green chiles, chopped
1 can stewed tomatoes, optional
1 tsp. ground cumin
1 tsp. chili powder
1/2 tsp. salt
1/2 tsp. pepper
2 Tbs. butter, melted
2 cups buttermilk
1 egg, beaten
1 cup cornmeal
1 tsp. baking soda
1/2 tsp salt

Sauté onion and garlic in a little oil until soft. Add beans, chiles, stewed tomatoes, spices, salt and pepper and simmer 5 minutes. Pour into an 8"x 8" pan or deep oval baking dish.

Mix cornbread by combining melted butter, buttermilk and egg. Then mix in dry ingredients. Pour over beans and bake for 30 - 40 minutes, uncovered, at 425° or until bread is golden. Serves 4 - 6.

This is a variation of Tennessee Corn Pone – something we've enjoyed from friends Karen and Tony, in Seneca Rocks. We like it served with mashed potatoes and sautéed spinach.

VEGETARIAN QUICHE

1 9" deep dish pie crust
3 eggs
1 1/4 cups milk
2 Tbs. flour
1/4 tsp. salt
1/8 tsp. black pepper
1/2 tsp. dried basil

Filling Suggestions:

   sautéed onions and garlic
   sautéed mushrooms
   sautéed bell peppers
   fresh spinach, wilted
   sliced fresh tomatoes
   grated cheese (Cheddar, Jack, Swiss, etc.)
   chopped cooked broccoli
   chopped green onions and green chiles
   grated zucchini, squash and/or carrots
   avocados

   Choose your fillings (use anything you like - this is a
time to be creative). Place 1 1/2 cups of filling in the pie
crust. Mix eggs, milk, flour and seasonings with a whisk.
Pour over filling and bake at 375° for 45 minutes or until
pie has set. Enjoy. Serves 6 - 8.

MARY ANN'S BROCCOLI PIE

This recipe is "easy as pie." It's like a quiche, but it makes it's own crust.

2 cups chopped fresh broccoli and/or cauliflower
1 Tbs. butter or margarine
1/2 cup chopped onion
1/2 cup chopped bell pepper (green, red or yellow)
1 cup shredded cheese (Cheddar, Swiss or Jack)
1 1/2 cups milk
3/4 cup flour sifted with 1/2 tsp. baking powder
3 eggs
Salt and pepper to taste

Preheat oven to 400°.
Steam broccoli until tender.
In a skillet, sauté onion and pepper in butter until cooked. Mix vegetables in a greased 10-inch pie plate with the cheese.
In a bowl, beat remaining ingredients until smooth and pour over the vegetables. Bake for 35 - 40 minutes until brown.

120

CHICKEN

There must be a million ways to
cook chicken; here are our favorites.

Creative Cooking

Following directions on a recipe is important. But, it's funny how six different people can follow the same recipe and the dish can come out tasting a little different every time. (That has happened at the cafe more than once.)

We wrote these recipes for you to follow, but if you want to add a little more of this or a little less of that, do it. (When cooking for ourselves, we usually add more garlic to every recipe.) If you don't care for an ingredient in a recipe - don't be afraid to substitute. Individualize your cooking. It should be fun. The more you enjoy cooking, the better your food will taste. Adding a little love makes everything you do shine.

BONNIE'S CEYLONESE CHICKEN

1 medium onion
5 cloves garlic
3 Tbs. fresh ginger, grated
1 tsp. cinnamon
1 tsp. crushed red peppers
1/3 cup fresh cilantro
1 Tbs. curry powder
1 tsp. salt
2 Tbs. vegetable oil
6 boneless, skinless chicken breasts
1 14 oz. can coconut milk
1 cup chicken broth
1 tsp. turmeric

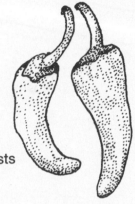

Using a food processor, blend onion, garlic, ginger, cinnamon, peppers, cilantro, curry and salt. Rub paste over chicken and marinate at least 2 hours.

In a large skillet, sear chicken in oil over high heat about two minutes. Remove chicken and add coconut milk and broth to the skillet. Stir in turmeric and return chicken to the skillet. Simmer for 15 - 20 minutes, until chicken is fully cooked. Serve over rice – basmati is an excellent choice.

This could soon become a favorite dish at your house. Make extra paste and keep it in the freezer for a fast (but great) dinner for another night.

This recipe came from two of my dearest friends, Bonnie and Ron. I have them to blame for my insatiable cravings for Indonesian and Indian foods.
MBG

M.B.'s GINGER CHICKEN

2 Tbs. vegetable oil
4 boneless, skinless chicken breasts
1 large onion, chopped
4 cloves garlic, chopped
2 carrots, peeled and chopped
1/4 cup fresh grated ginger
1/2 tsp. cinnamon
1/4 tsp. ground cardamom
1 Tbs. vegetable broth powder
2 tsp. black pepper
1 tsp. turmeric
1/4 tsp. cayenne pepper
1 tsp. salt
1/3 cup water
1 28 oz. can chopped tomatoes
1 10 oz. pkg. frozen peas

Cut chicken into 1-inch cubes. Heat oil in a large skillet and brown chicken on both sides, remove from pan. Then add onions and garlic, sauté 2 minutes then add carrots, ginger, and spices. Stir and sauté until veggies are tender. Add water and tomatoes with their juice. Return chicken, add peas and simmer until meat is thoroughly cooked. Serve with basmati rice. To make this dish vegetarian, substitute tofu for the chicken.

Indian foods are some of our favorites at White Grass. This recipe came about as I wanted to make a dish with cardamom. It's one of my favorite spices. MBG

CHICKEN BYZANTINE

Our friend and guest chef extraordinare, George Mikedes, made this and brought the house down in February of 1996.

1 1/2 cups sliced onions
2 Tbs. dried tarragon
Salt and pepper to taste
2 1/2 - 3 lbs. skinless chicken pieces
1/2 cup honey
1/4 cup orange juice
2 Tbs. butter
Dash of garlic powder
1/2 cup sliced almonds
3/4 cup golden raisins
1/4 cup pine nuts
1/4 cup fresh chopped parsley
1/2 cup dry Vermouth

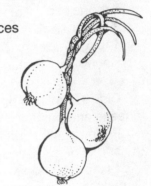

In a large roasting pan, lay sliced onions and sprinkle with tarragon. Season chicken with salt and pepper and place on onions. Mix honey and o.j. and pour over chicken. Bake at 350° for 45 minutes, basting and turning chicken occasionally.

In a saucepan, melt butter. Add garlic powder and almonds and stir until nuts are light brown. Remove from heat.

In another saucepan, heat Vermouth. Add raisins, pine nuts and parsley until raisins are plump or liquid is absorbed. Mix with almonds and spoon over chicken. Serve with rice pilaf.

CHICKEN CORDON BLEU

1/4 lb. hard salami
1/4 lb. baked deli ham
3/4 cup chopped green onions
1/2 lb. grated Monterey Jack cheese
1/4 cup chopped fresh parsley
6 boneless, skinless chicken breasts
2 eggs, beaten
1 pkg. Shake n' Bake or chicken seasoning
Round toothpicks

Dice salami and ham, mix with green onions, grated cheese and parsley for the filling.

Pound chicken until thin and flat, about 1/4 inch. Pack a handful of filling and set in the middle of the breast. Wrap sides around and secure with toothpicks. Sometimes this is tricky, just use a lot of toothpicks.

Brush with beaten egg, then dust with Shake n' Bake. In a 350° oven, bake 45 minutes. Don't forget to remove the toothpicks before serving to your guests.

This is the best cordon bleu recipe we've found. We like to serve it with hot rice, broccoli and a Hollandaise Sauce.

LOWFAT LOVE CHICKEN
In Sundried Tomato and Cream Sauce

1/2 cup sundried tomatoes
1/2 cup dry white wine
6 oz. fat free or lowfat cream cheese, room temp.
3/4 cup boiling water
4 skinless, boneless, chicken breasts
1 Tbs. butter
6 green onions, chopped
1 clove garlic, minced
1/4 tsp. dried basil
1/4 tsp. black pepper

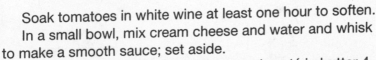

Soak tomatoes in white wine at least one hour to soften.
In a small bowl, mix cream cheese and water and whisk
to make a smooth sauce; set aside.
Cut chicken into bite-sized pieces and sauté in butter 4
minutes, until mostly cooked and remove from pan. Sauté
onions and garlic in pan then add cream cheese, wine and
tomatoes. Mix and simmer two minutes. Add chicken, basil
and pepper and simmer 5 minutes. Serves 4. Instead of the
cream cheese sauce, you can use the Garlic Bechamel
Sauce on page 157.

Our friend Elizabeth Gillespie gave us this recipe
with the instructions to serve it with "wild rice,
candlelight and the one you love." (That's why we
call it Love Chicken). We made it lowfat by using fat
free cream cheese instead of cream to make the
sauce. Enjoy the richness and don't feel guilty.

CHICKEN ENCHILADAS

2 Tbs. vegetable oil
6 cloves garlic, chopped
2 medium onions, chopped
1 4.5 oz. can green chiles
3 cups cooked chicken, shredded
1 large can crushed tomatoes
2 roasted, pureed peppers* (Ancho, Bell,
  Chipolte – or your favorite)
2 tsp. ground cumin
1/2 tsp. salt
1/2 tsp. black pepper
1 dozen corn tortillas
1 1/2 cups grated Cheddar or Jack cheese

In a skillet, sauté 3 cloves of garlic and onions in 1 Tbs. oil until soft. Then add canned chiles and chicken. Mix well and remove from heat.

In a saucepan, make sauce by sautéing remaining garlic in oil until lightly golden, then add crushed tomatoes and pureed roasted peppers, cumin, salt and pepper. Stir until well blended and simmer until heated through.

Place a large spoonful of chicken onto each tortilla. Roll up and lay them in a casserole dish. Pour sauce over enchiladas, cover with grated cheese and bake for 30 minutes at 350°. Serve with sour cream, Mexican White Sauce, fresh tomatoes and lettuce, chopped cilantro, or any of your favorite accompaniments. Serves 6.

* See directions for roasting peppers on page 24.

CHICKEN FAJITAS

4 boneless, skinless, chicken breasts
1 Tbs. vegetable oil
4 Tbs. lime juice
2 tsp. ground cumin
1 large onion, sliced
2 green bell peppers, sliced
1 dozen large flour tortillas

Marinate chicken in oil, lime juice and cumin at least 15 minutes. Cook chicken on grill or in a heavy skillet, cool slightly and slice into long, thin strips. Remove chicken from skillet and sauté onion and pepper. Wrap tortillas in foil and warm them in the oven.

Serve chicken and veggies hot and with lots of extras so each person can make their own fajita. Have plenty of salsa, lettuce, shredded cheese, sour cream and guacamole on hand and maybe some wild hot sauce to heat things up. Serves 4 - 6.

MARINATED GRILLED CHICKEN

1 8 oz. can tomato sauce
1/2 cup olive oil
1/2 cup orange juice
1/4 cup red wine vinegar
3 cloves garlic, minced
1/2 tsp. whole black peppercorns
1 1/2 tsp. dried oregano
6 chicken breasts or a combination of
    thighs, wings and legs (3 pounds)

Combine all ingredients, except chicken, in a bowl and mix well. Add chicken and marinate in fridge overnight. Cook chicken on a charcoal or gas grill until minutes from being done, then brush with glaze. Grill for another 3 - 4 minutes. Serves 6.

HONEY MUSTARD GLAZE

1/4 cup honey
1/2 tsp. dry mustard

Mix both ingredients together in a bowl or cup. Brush on chicken generously when it is minutes from being done.

CHICKEN ON THE HOT SIDE

Local Thai lovers, "Chef" Jeff and Ruth Melnick have prepared this awesome recipe for a record breaking crowd at the cafe. It's hot and spicy and so easy to make. Try using catfish instead of chicken if you like.

- 2 Tbs. Thai green curry paste*
- 2 Tbs. canola oil
- 2 boneless, skinless chicken breasts (1 pound)
- 3 Tbs. fish sauce*
- 1 14 oz. can coconut milk*
- 5 Tbs. fresh lime juice
- 1 cup frozen peas

In a wok or deep skillet, sauté curry paste in oil for 4 minutes. Cut chicken into 1-inch pieces and add to wok. Add 2 Tbs. fish sauce and stir until meat is barely cooked. Add coconut milk, rest of the fish sauce, lime juice and peas. Let simmer until boiling. Serve in a bowl over jasmine* rice. Enough for 4.

* These items cannot be found in your average grocery. You need to go to an Asian or Indian food store.

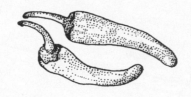

131

CURRIED CHICKEN

2 medium onions, chopped
1 Tbs. margarine
3 baking apples, peeled and chopped
2 11 oz. cans cream of mushroom soup
2 cups whole milk
6 boneless, skinless chicken breasts
1 tsp. cayenne pepper
2 tsp. curry powder

Sauté chopped onions until tender in margarine, then add apples. Stir in soup and milk until you have a creamy sauce.

Place chicken breasts in a 9 x 13 baking pan. Sprinkle with cayenne and curry and pour sauce over chicken. Cover with foil and bake 30 minutes at 350° then remove foil and bake another 20 minutes. Serve with Indian Potatoes and Peas and Chipatis.

We just love this dish, a recipe from Eira Patnik, a former guest chef. It is easy - especially for a big crowd. If you want to make it stretch further, cut the chicken into chunks or add some tofu, cut into chunks.

PESTO CHICKEN WITH PASTA

2 – 3 boneless, skinless, chicken breasts
1 Tbs. olive oil
2 cloves garlic, minced
3 Tbs. pesto (see page 106)
1 lb. spaghetti or linguini
1 Tbs. butter
Parmesan cheese for garnish

Cut chicken into 1- inch cubes. Heat oil in a skillet, add garlic and chicken and sauté until chicken is cooked through. Stir in 1 Tbs. of the pesto and mix well.

Meanwhile, boil water in a large pot and cook the pasta. While noodles are draining, melt butter in the pasta pot. Return noodles to the pot and toss. Add remaining pesto and mix well. Be careful not to pulverize the pasta. Arrange pasta on plates and top with chicken. Serve immediately with plenty of Parmesan; serves 4.

Another fabulous recipe from Richmond friends,
Jenny and Chris Laude.

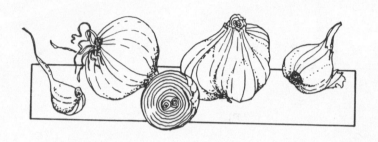

We'd like to take this moment, and space, to honor the thing we hold dearest to us, as cooks. The thing that is embraced by nearly every recipe in this book. (Excluding the desserts.) The very thing that, after close contact, stays with you, like a beautiful memory. The pungent, yet ·sweet – garlic. Our lives would be empty without you.

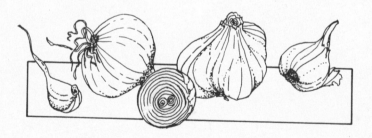

FISH AND SEAFOOD

These are some of our easiest
and most creative dishes. Fish is
so good for you and really easy to
cook. We're hooked on it.

Even More Love Letters

"A 'ski homey' flavor is generated throughout the cookbook which makes it warm, inviting, and friendly for use. Great sayings like 'eat for living in the mountains' makes for great reading. I find something new everytime I look up a recipe. Cheers!"

Jeanne Holmes
Norwich, Vermont

"While staying at the Hill House in Davis, we stumbled across your cookbook and pounced on the opportunity to obtain it for ourselves. We love it. Everything we have prepared has been very tasty, as well as easy and visually appealing. Kudos to a great collection of recipes."

Tom Savelle
Seattle, Washington

"Just spent a great weekend in Canaan Valley. I got an autographed copy of the White Grass Cafe Cookbook which I read from cover to cover on my way home. I'll be busy in the kitchen for the rest of the winter! Thank you so much for such an absolutely wonderful place filled with absolutely wonderful people. You do yourselves proud."

Lisa Gillogly

TROUT PROVENCAL

French spices have inspired this light and very flavorful dish. Herbes de Provence is a delicate blend of spices like thyme, rosemary, savory, tarragon and basil. Annie Snyder brought us Herbes de Provence from France and this is what we did with them.

4 trout fillets
1 tsp. Herbes de Provence
2 Tbs. butter
3 cloves garlic, minced
Juice from one lemon

Lay fillets on a foil-covered baking pan. Sauté garlic in butter and drizzle over each fish. Then sprinkle 1/4 tsp. of herbs on each fish. Squeeze lemon juice on the fillets and bake at 450° for seven minutes. Be careful not to overcook the fish or it will be dry.

CHILE TROUT

Having a trout farm just down the road, we've come up with some great ways to prepare this wonderful delicate fish. This is probably the most popular.

1 onion, chopped
1 Tbs. oil
4 cloves garlic
1 roasted red pepper*
1 bunch fresh cilantro
2 dried Ancho chilies, soaked in water till soft
3 Tbs. fresh lime juice
1/4 tsp. salt
6 whole trout, filleted
2 limes, cut into wedges

Pureé onion, oil, peppers, garlic and cilantro in a food processor, add lime juice and salt. Rub paste over fish. Bake at 450° for 10 – 15 minutes, or until fish is flaky. Don't overbake. Serve with lime wedges. This chile paste works well with Catfish, or any other whitefish and can also be made ahead of time and stored in the fridge or freezer.

*See page 24 for information on roasting peppers.

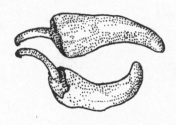

COUSCOUS STUFFED TROUT

4 fresh trout fillets
3/4 cup couscous
3/4 cup boiling water
1 Tbs. olive oil
1/4 cup green onion, chopped
3 cloves garlic, minced
1/2 cup chopped fresh mushrooms
2 Tbs. fresh parsley, chopped
Salt and pepper to taste

Lay fillets on a foiled baking sheet. In a bowl, pour water over couscous and cover; let sit until grains have soaked up the water (5 minutes). In the meantime, heat oil in a skillet and sauté garlic and onion for two minutes, then add mushrooms and parsley. Cook another two minutes and cool. Mix vegetables and couscous and season with salt and pepper. Spoon filling over each fillet and "pack" it on. Bake at 450° for 10 - 15 minutes. Serve with sauce below.

CREAMY GARLIC MUSHROOM SAUCE

2 Tbs. butter or margarine
2 Tbs. flour
3 cloves garlic, minced
8 oz. mushrooms, chopped
2 cups milk
Salt and pepper to taste

In a saucepan, heat butter over medium heat. Stir in flour and keep stirring while adding garlic and mushrooms. Cook 3 or 4 minutes, then add milk, still stirring. Simmer until sauce thickens and season with salt and pepper.

CREAMY SMOKED TROUT
AND PEAS OVER PASTA

1 8 oz. pkg. non-fat or lowfat cream cheese, softened
1 cup boiling water
1/4 cup Parmesan cheese
8 oz. smoked trout pieces
1 10 oz. pkg. frozen peas
2 cloves garlic
1 Tbs. butter
1 lb. fettuccini or other pasta

To make sauce, pour boiling water over cream cheese in a medium saucepan and stir until smooth. Add Parmesan, mix. Keep sauce warm over low heat and add trout and peas, stir gently.

Cook pasta according to package directions. Sauté garlic in butter and toss with pasta. Arrange hot pasta on plates and spoon on sauce. Garnish with thinly sliced lemon and Parmesan. Serves 4.

This is similar to our fettucini alfrieda sauce. The addition of smoked trout makes a wonderfully rich taste. Using non-fat cream cheese makes this dish healthier but still rich.

SESAME CRUSTED GROUPER

1 - 1 1/2 lbs. fish fillets
1 cup sesame seeds
1/4 cup flour
1 egg beaten with 1 Tbs. water
1/4 cup vegetable oil

Toast sesame seeds in a dry skillet over medium heat for 1 - 3 minutes (don't burn them). Dredge fish in flour, then egg, then sesame seeds. Pan fry in oil for at least 3 minutes on each side or until done. The thicker the fillet, the longer you will have to cook it. Serve with rice and dipping sauce, below. Serves 4.

HOT ORIENTAL DIPPING SAUCE

3/4 cup soy sauce
1/2 cup water
1/4 cup sugar
1 Tbs. white vinegar
1 Tbs. toasted sesame oil
12 slices fresh ginger
2 cloves garlic, minced
1 tsp. lemon juice
1 tsp. Tabasco or hot sauce
2 tsp. cornstarch
1/4 cup cold water

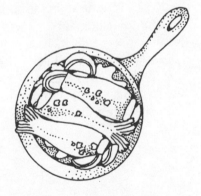

Combine all ingredients except cornstarch and cold water in a saucepan, simmer 5 minutes. Dissolve cornstarch in cold water then add to pan. Cook, stirring constantly for 1 minute. Serve warm with fish, veggie cakes, appetizers – anything.

PEPPERED SALMON
With Lemon Butter

A superb recipe from Nancy Krough, owner and head chef of The Cheat River Inn. (Our other favorite restaurant.)

1 cup vegetable oil
1/3 cup soy sauce
1/3 cup lemon juice
1 Tbs. fresh or 1 tsp. dried dill
1 cup freshly ground black pepper
4 7-8 oz. salmon fillets, skin removed
Sea salt to taste
1/3 cup fresh squeezed lemon juice
1/2 lb. butter, (unsalted), softened

Preheat grill or broiler to maximum heat.
Make a marinade by mixing oil, soy sauce, lemon juice, and dill. Marinate fish for 5 minutes, remove and drain on paper towels. Put black pepper on a plate and coat fish on both sides.
Mix salt, lemon juice and butter, set aside.
With a heavy cloth, oil the grill and lay the fish on it. Cook until done, Remove to warm plates and top with lemon butter. Serves 4.

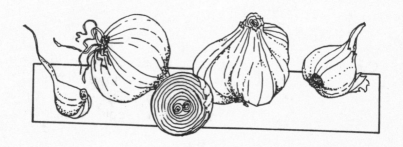

CAJUN CATFISH

This recipe is easy, easy, easy -- and it tastes pretty darn good too. You don't have to limit yourself to catfish. The Cajun spices also blend well with trout, shrimp, grouper or redfish.

    4 catfish fillets
    4 tsp. Cajun seasoning

Rub each fillet with a teaspoon of seasoning paste. Bake at 450° for 6 - 10 minutes, depending on the thickness of the fish. Fish is done when it flakes. Serves 4.

CAJUN SEASONING

    3 tsp. salt   4 cloves garlic, minced
    4 tsp. paprika   3 Tbs. chopped onion
    3 tsp. black pepper   1 1/2 tsp. dried thyme
    1 1/2 tsp. dried oregano   1 1/2 tsp. cayenne pepper

Combine all ingredients in a food processor. Blend until a paste forms. Store in an airtight container in the refrigerator.

SEAFOOD GUMBO

This dish is intended as an entrée, but also makes a great soup. Just add a little broth and adjust the seasonings to your taste.

1 cup chopped onion
4 cloves chopped garlic
1 cup chopped mushrooms
1 cup chopped celery
1 cup tomato puree
1/2 cup canned tomatoes, drained
1 10 oz. pkg. frozen okra *(in freezer)*
5 bay leaves
1/4 tsp. cayenne pepper
1/2 lb. raw shrimp, peeled
1/2 lb. whitefish fillets, cut into chunks = *chicken*
2 6 1/2 oz. cans chopped clams with juice
Salt and pepper to taste
2 Tbs. filé (add just before serving)

Sauté onion, garlic, mushrooms and celery in a small amount of oil in a large saucepan. Add tomatoes, okra and spices and heat through. Then add seafood and fish and simmer until all seafood is cooked, but not overcooked (about 10 - 15 minutes). Stir in filé and serve over hot rice. Serves 4 - 6.

RED CURRY SHARK

Serving shark has generated some interesting conversation at the cafe. It's been said that eating shark gives men increased sexual potency.

- 1 Tbs. vegetable oil
- 3 cloves garlic, minced
- 2 lbs. shark fillets
- 1 14 oz. cans coconut milk*
- 1 Tbs. Thai red curry paste*
- 2 Tbs. soy sauce

Cut shark into 1 inch cubes. Sauté oil and garlic in a large skillet. Add shark and cook for 3 - 4 minutes. Then add coconut milk, curry paste and soy sauce, mix well. Simmer at least 5 minutes but don't overcook the shark. Serve over white or basmati rice. A beautiful vegetable stir fry goes nicely with this for an entrée. Serves 4 - 6.

*These items available at Asian and Indian food markets.

SCALLOPS SIAM

If scallops aren't available, you can use a variety of fish for this dish. We like shrimp, catfish, swordfish or grouper.

- 1 Tbs. vegetable oil
- 3 cloves garlic, minced
- 2 lbs. sea scallops
- 2 14 oz.cans coconut milk*
- 1 Tbs. Thai red curry paste*
- 2 Tbs. soy sauce
- 1 tsp. fresh parsley, chopped

In a large skillet, sauté garlic in oil over medium heat. Then add scallops. Cook for two minutes then add curry paste, milk and soy sauce. Stir and simmer about 5 minutes. Don't overcook the scallops. Stir in parsley. Serve over white rice (basmati tastes real good). Enough for 4 - 6 people.

> This recipe is from our friend, Debbie Harkrader. It has been said by more than one person that this is the best dish ever served at the cafe.

* Available at Asian or Indian food markets.

WHITE GRASS
SKI TOURING CENTER

SHRIMP PRIMAVERA

This is a "suped up" version of scampi from Colleen Laffey. It's great with rice or pasta, a big salad and a crusty bread.

2 pounds large fresh shrimp
6 cloves garlic, minced
1/2 stick butter – not margarine
1/4 cup dry white wine
Juice of two lemons
1 Tbs. vegetable oil
1 cup carrots, julienned
1 red bell pepper, sliced thin
1 bunch broccoli, cut in pieces
1 bunch green onions, chopped
1/2 lb. fresh snow peas
1 tsp. dried tarragon
1/2 cup chopped parsley

You'll need two skillets – one for veggies and one for shrimp. In one skillet, melt butter over medium-high heat and sauté garlic for one minute. Add shrimp and cook 2 - 3 minutes. Add wine and lemon juice and simmer until shrimp is pink. Don't overcook.

In the other skillet, sauté carrots, broccoli, green onions and red pepper in oil for 2 - 3 minutes, then add snow peas, cook another minute. Toss the veggies and shrimp together with tarragon and parsley. Serves 4 - 6.

SHRIMP AND CRAB ETOUFFE

Excellent cajun cuisine, this is one of our most special dishes at White Grass. It looks involved but is definitely worth it.

1 large onion
6 green onions
1 large green pepper
1 large red bell pepper
3 ribs celery
3/4 cup chopped parsley
6 cloves garlic
1/2 stick butter
3 Tbs. flour
6 cups water

1 Tbs. seafood seasoning
1/2 tsp. cayenne pepper
2 tsp. salt
1/2 tsp. ground black pepper
1/2 tsp. ground white pepper
1 Tbs. vegetable boullion
1 1/2 lbs. large raw shrimp, shells on
1 lb. crab meat

In a food processor, finely chop onions, peppers, celery, parsley and garlic.

Melt butter in a large pot over med-high heat. Add flour to make a roux and stir constantly until it becomes peanut butter colored. Be careful not to burn the roux. Add the chopped vegetables and let them cook until soft, about 30 minutes. Remember to stir occasionally so they don't stick.

In the meantime, peel and devein shrimp. Save the shells and make a stock by boiling them in the water and seafood seasoning for 8 - 10 minutes, then strain.

When the veggies are done, add the stock and stir. Simmer, then add the remaining seasonings. You may want to adjust them to your own taste. About 15 minutes before you are ready to eat, add the crab and shrimp. Cook until shrimp are pink and tender, don't overcook – they will get tough. This dish goes best over hot fluffy rice. Serves 6.

GREEK SHRIMP OVER FETTUCCINI

Serve this dish to your favorite people, they'll love you.

5 Tbs. butter
6 cloves garlic, minced
1 cup chopped green onions
2/3 cup chopped fresh parsley
1 large can whole peeled tomatoes
1 tsp. dried basil
1 tsp. dried oregano
1/2 cup dry white wine
1 lb. fresh large shrimp, peeled and cleaned
1/2 lb. crumbled feta cheese
1 lb. fettuccini noodles

In a large saucepan, melt 2 Tbs. butter. Sauté 3 cloves garlic and onions until tender, add parsley. Add tomatoes (crush them with your hands) and juice and herbs. Gently simmer until liquid reduces (15 minutes) and stir in wine. This sauce can be made ahead of time, even the night before.

Cook pasta according to package directions. When noodles are done, sauté shrimp in 3 cloves minced garlic and 3 Tbs. butter until pink. Add shrimp to heated tomato sauce and stir in half of the feta cheese. Do not overcook the sauce or the shrimp will get dry and tough.

Place noodles on plates and spoon on sauce. Garnish with remaining feta. Serves 4 heartily.

SHRIMP SCAMPI

This is your basic scampi recipe. A shrimp lovers favorite. It's worth it to splurge on good shrimp for this dish. Remember, a meal is only as good as its ingredients.

2 pounds large, fresh shrimp
6 cloves garlic, minced
1 stick butter (margarine won't do)
1/4 cup dry white wine
1/3 cup chopped fresh parsley
Juice from 2 lemons

Peel and devein shrimp. In a large skillet, sauté garlic in butter over medium heat for one minute then add shrimp. Sauté another two minutes then add wine, parsley and lemon juice. Simmer until shrimp is cooked - but not over cooked. Serve with pasta or rice, enough for 4 - 6 people.

LINGUINI WITH WHITE CLAM SAUCE

Talk about quick and easy – this is a great dinner you can throw together at the last minute.

2 Tbs. olive oil
1/2 cup finely chopped yellow onion
1/2 cup chopped green onion
4 cloves garlic
1/3 cup dry white wine
2 Tbs. lemon juice
2 tsp. dried basil
1 tsp. dried thyme
1/2 tsp. crushed red pepper flakes
2 6 1/2 oz. cans chopped clams
4 Tbs. parsley
1/4 cup grated Parmesan
1 lb. linguini noodles

In a large saucepan, sauté onions and garlic in olive oil until just tender. Add wine, lemon juice and herbs, cook for two minutes. Then add clams, with juice and parsley. Simmer on low heat until bubbling.

Cook pasta according to package directions. Ladle sauce over cooked noodles. Serve in bowls and sprinkle with pepper flakes and Parmesan cheese. Serves 4.

SEAFOOD PESTO ALFREDO

1 8 oz. cream cheese, softened
1 cup boiling water
1/4 cup Parmesan cheese
2 Tbs. prepared pesto, page 106
1/2 lb. raw shrimp, peeled and deveined
1 lb. fresh salmon fillet, cut into chunks
3 cloves garlic, minced
2 Tbs. butter
1 lb. fettuccini or favorite pasta

In a saucepan, pour boiling water over cream cheese and stir until smooth. Add Parmesan and pesto, mix well.

Cook pasta according to package directions. While it is cooking, cut salmon into bite-sized chunks. Then sauté garlic in butter and add shrimp and salmon. Cook until just done. Don't overcook. Add to sauce and stir, keep warm until the pasta is done. Serve sauce over pasta, making sure to give equal amounts of shrimp and salmon. Serves 4 as a meal with salad and a crusty French bread.

CRAB CAKES

2 pounds crab meat
1/3 cup onion, finely chopped
1 cup breadcrumbs
1/2 tsp. dried mustard
1 tsp. Worchestershire sauce
2 Tbs. chopped fresh parsley
1 tsp. Old Bay or other seafood seasoning
2 eggs, beaten
1 1/2 Tbs. pureed roasted red peppers*
1/4 cup vegetable oil

Pick through crab meat to remove any shell fragments. Stir in remaining ingredients, except for oil. Mix well and form into 12 patties. Sauté in oil until golden. Serve with Roasted Red Pepper Sauce (below).

ROASTED RED PEPPER SAUCE

1 cup sour cream
1/3 cup mayonnaise
1 Tbs. lemon juice
1 tsp. chopped parsley
2 Tbs. pickle relish
1/4 cup pureed roasted red peppers*

Mix all ingredients until well blended. Serve on the side of crab cakes. This can be made in advance and chilled.

* See page 24 for instructions on roasting peppers.

SALMON CAKES

1 16 oz. can pink salmon
1 cup breadcrumbs *
1 bunch green onions, chopped fine
2 cloves garlic, minced
1 tsp. dried dill weed
1 tsp. fresh chopped parsley
1 egg, beaten
Juice from 1 lemon

Open can of salmon and pick out any large bones or skin. Mix well with remaining ingredients. (You can use your hands). Shape into patties and sauté in a little oil (3 Tbs.) until browned on both sides. Keep warm in the oven until all cakes are cooked. Serve with big lemon wedges and a huge salad.

*You can use leftover baked or mashed potatoes instead of breadcrumbs. It tastes great and is a good way to clean out the fridge.

THAI-STYLE FISH CAKES

Any type of fish is suitable for this dish. Whiting, cod, perch or more expensive catfish or grouper can be used.

1 lb. raw fish fillets
3 cloves minced garlic
1 tsp. fresh grated ginger
6 green onions, chopped
1/2 cup chopped fresh cilantro
1 Tbs. soy sauce
1 egg, beaten
2 Tbs. flour
Oil for frying

Chop fish or pulse it in a food processor. Mix with garlic, ginger, onions, cilantro, soy sauce and egg. Shape into patties and refrigerate for 30 minutes. Heat skillet with 3 Tbs. oil, dredge patties in flour and sauté, until brown on both sides. Serve with Hot Oriental Dipping Sauce, on page 141.

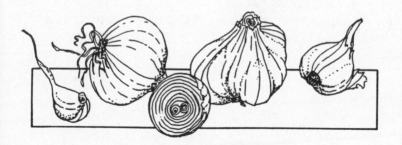

SEAFOOD LASAGNA

1 medium onion, chopped
1 Tbs. olive oil
2 15 oz. containers cottage or ricotta cheese
1 10 oz. pkg. frozen chopped spinach,
     thawed & squeezed
1/4 cup Parmesan cheese
3 eggs, beaten
1 tsp. dried basil
1/4 tsp. black pepper
1 lb. shrimp, peeled and deveined
8 oz. fresh crabmeat
1 6.5 oz. can chopped clams with their juice
1 box lasagna noodles
1 1/2 cups grated mozzarella
1 recipe Garlic Bechamel Sauce

Sauté onion in oil and mix with ricotta, spinach,
Parmesan, eggs, basil and pepper, beat well.

Make Garlic Bechamel Sauce (see page 157) and add
shrimp, crab and clams, simmer until shrimp is cooked,
about 10 minutes.

Assemble lasagna by layering sauce, noodles, filling,
shredded mozzarella then sauce, in a 9 x 13" pan. Cover
with foil and bake at 350° for 45 minutes, remove foil and
bake an additional 15 minutes. Remove from oven and let
sit at least 20 minutes before cutting and serving.

White Grass Cafe

GARLIC BECHAMEL SAUCE

4 Tbs. butter or margarine
6 cloves garlic
4 Tbs. flour
2 cups milk
Salt and pepper to taste

In a two-quart saucepan, heat butter over medium-high heat. Add garlic and sauté two minutes. Add flour, stirring constantly, and cook until mixture begins to turn light brown. Add milk, still stirring, and lower heat. Simmer until sauce is desired thickness. Season.

FISHERMAN'S PAN STEW

2 Tbs. butter
3-4 shallots, roughly chopped
1 clove garlic, chopped
12 mushroom stems
1 bay leaf

6 black peppercorns
1 Tbs. dried thyme
1/2 cup white wine
3 cups heavy cream
1 Tbs. dry mustard

In a large, heavy saucepan, heat butter until foamy. Add shallots, garlic and mushroom stems and cook until soft. Add the bay leaf, peppercorns and thyme. Stir. Add the wine and reduce until almost a glaze. Add the cream and reduce until thick enough to coat a spoon. Whisk in the mustard and then strain through a fine mesh strainer. Keep warm and continue with other directions.

1 lb. fettuccini
4 Tbs. butter
1 1/2 lb. asst. fish and shellfish, cut into 1/2" pieces
1 leek, cleaned and sliced into very thin julienne
1 carrot, sliced into very thin julienne
1 stalk celery, sliced into very thin julienne
12 mushroom caps, sliced
1/4 cup white wine

Cook pasta and drain.

In a large skillet, heat butter and add raw fish and stir. Add all the vegetables and stir evenly. Add wine and simmer a moment. Now add cream sauce and pasta and toss together. Lift the mixture into heated bowls. Garnish with Parmesan cheese if desired.

Nancy Krough, owner of The Cheat River Inn in Elkins, WV, generously gave us this recipe. We love to eat at her restaurant and this is one of our favorite entrées there.

DESSERTS

We take pride in the fact that all our desserts are homemade. These are tried and true – simple to make and simply delicious to eat.

WHITE GRASS OATMEAL COOKIES

3/4 cup margarine (softened)
3/4 cup honey
1 egg
2 Tbs. water
1 tsp. vanilla
1/2 cup unbleached white flour
1/2 cup whole wheat pastry flour
1 tsp. salt
1/2 tsp. baking soda
1 1/2 tsp. cinnamon
1 tsp. allspice
3 cups rolled oats
1 cup raisins
1 cup roasted sunflower seeds

Preheat oven to 350°. Cream margarine and honey. Add egg, water and vanilla. Stir in flour, salt, baking soda and spices. Add oats, raisins, and sunflower seeds – mix well. Drop by rounded teaspoons onto an ungreased cookie sheet, about 1 inch apart. Bake 10 - 15 minutes, or until almost no imprint remains when touched. Cool slightly before removing from sheet. Makes 3 dozen.

What a great trail snack. These are a cafe
favorite since its inception.

OUR FAMOUS CHOCOLATE CHIP COOKIES

1 1/3 cup margarine, softened
1 cup granulated sugar
1 cup brown sugar, packed
2 eggs
2 tsp. vanilla
2 cups all-purpose flour
1 1/2 cups whole wheat pastry flour
1 tsp. baking soda
1 tsp. salt
12 oz. semisweet chocolate chips

Heat oven to 350°. Cream margarine and sugars. Mix in eggs and vanilla and beat until creamy. Stir in remaining ingredients, mixing well. Drop by rounded spoonfuls onto ungreased cookie sheet 2 inches apart. Bake 8 - 10 minutes or until light brown. Cool slightly before removing from cookie sheet.

We make these cookies as big as your face. It's a lot of cookie, but most people can handle it. As Mary McHugh says, "One cookie serves 4."

MOLASSES SUGAR COOKIES

1 1/2 sticks butter or margarine
1 cup sugar
1/4 cup molasses
1 egg
2 cups all purpose flour
2 tsp. baking soda
1/2 tsp. ground cloves
1/2 tsp. ground ginger
1 tsp. cinnamon
1/2 tsp. salt

Melt butter in a medium saucepan over low heat. Remove from heat, add sugar, molasses and egg, beat well. Add flour, soda, spices and salt, mix well and chill.

Form into 1-inch balls and roll in sugar. Place on greased cookie sheet and bake at 375° for 8-10 minutes. Makes three dozen cookies.

ALMOND BISCOTTI

1 cup whole almonds, chopped
3/4 cup sliced almonds
2 3/4 cups all-purpose flour
1 cup sugar
1/2 tsp. salt
1 tsp. baking powder
2 tsp. anise seed
Grated zest of 1 lemon, 1 lime, 1 orange
3 eggs plus 3 egg yolks
1 tsp. vanilla
1 tsp. anise oil or extract (optional)

Toast all almonds in a 350° oven for 3 minutes – being careful not to burn them; let cool.

In a large bowl, or mixer, combine flour, sugar, salt, baking powder, anise seed and fruit zests. In a separate bowl, lightly whisk eggs and extracts. Add eggs to the dry mixture and mix until the dough just comes together. Do not overmix. Lightly knead dough on a flat work surface – adding a little flour if needed.

Divide the dough into three equal parts and roll into logs, about 2-3 inches wide. Place 4 inches apart on a large greased baking sheet. Bake 45 minutes at 350° until lightly brown. Remove from oven and let cool for 10 minutes. Then slice logs into 3/4 inch pieces. Reduce oven to 300° and return cookies to the oven for 10 to 15 more minutes. Biscotti will not turn darker, but will become dry.

Cool and store in an airtight container. These cookies can also be dipped in coating chocolate for nut and chocolate lovers.

INCREDIBLE CARROT CAKE

1 1/2 cups whole wheat flour
3/4 cup all purpose flour
2 tsp. baking soda
2 tsp. cinnamon
1/2 tsp. salt
1/2 tsp. nutmeg
1/4 tsp. ground ginger
1 cup granulated sugar
1 cup brown sugar
1 cup buttermilk

3/4 cup vegetable oil
4 eggs
1/2 tsp. vanilla
1 8 oz. can crushed
    pineapple
1 lb. carrots, grated
1 cup chopped walnuts
1 cup flaked coconut
1/2 cup raisins

Combine flours, baking soda, salt and spices and set aside. In a large bowl, combine sugars, milk, oil, eggs and vanilla – blend well. Add flour, pineapple, carrots, walnuts, coconut and raisins. Bake at 350° in three greased and floured 8-inch round cake pans or two 10-inch pans for 30 minutes.

CREAM CHEESE FROSTING

2 Tbs. butter, softened
1 8 oz. pkg. cream cheese
1 16 oz. box confectioners sugar
1 tsp. vanilla
1 tsp. grated orange peel

Soften butter and cream cheese and beat with an electric mixer. Add sugar, vanilla and orange peel, beat until smooth.

Don't let this long list of ingredients fool you –
this cake is easy.
It's also the best carrot cake you'll ever eat!

PINEAPPLE UPSIDE DOWN CAKE

3 eggs, separated
1 cup white sugar
5 Tbs. pineapple juice
1 tsp. baking powder
1 cup flour
1/2 cup butter
1 cup brown sugar
1 16 oz. can sliced pineapple

Beat egg yolks and white sugar, add juice and baking powder, sift in flour. Beat egg whites until stiff and gently fold into batter.

In a 12-inch cast iron skillet, melt butter then add brown sugar, stir until blended. Arrange pineapple rings in skillet. (You can make this cake even more attractive by accenting the pineapple with marachino cherries and walnut or pecan halves).

Pour batter in skillet and bake at 350° for 20 minutes or until golden brown. Cool only 5 minutes and invert onto a cake plate.

This recipe is from my Dad's mother, Mabel Gwyer. She was Swedish and loved sweets. This is the best upside down cake I've ever eaten. MBG

GERRY'S CHOCOLATE CAKE

This is my mom's cake and my aunt's frosting. Two of the best recipes from two of the best cooks I know. MBG

2 1/4 cups sifted cake flour
1 tsp. baking soda
3/4 tsp. salt
2 cups brown sugar
1/2 cup margarine

1 tsp. vanilla
1 cup buttermilk
3 eggs
2 oz. unsweetened
   chocolate, melted

Sift together flour, soda and salt in a large bowl. Add brown sugar, margarine, vanilla and half the milk. Beat for two minutes on medium speed of a mixer. Add rest of the milk, eggs and chocolate. Beat 2 more minutes. Pour into two 9" round greased pans. Bake 30-35 minutes at 350°. Remove from oven and cool 10 minutes. Then remove cake from pans to cool completely, then frost.

MARTHA'S AUNT LOUISIE'S
CHOCOLATE FROSTING

5 egg yolks
1 cup milk
1 tsp. vanilla

2 1/2 cups sugar
4 oz. unsweetened
   chocolate

In a heavy bottomed saucepan or iron skillet, beat eggs and milk with a whisk, over low heat. Beat well and add vanilla, sugar and chocolate. Stir until chocolate is melted. Bring to a boil, stirring constantly until it spins a thread. Cool and beat until it reaches spreading consistancy.

166

SWEET POTATO CAKE

1 cup vegetable oil
2 cups sugar
4 eggs
1 cup all-purpose flour
1 cup whole wheat pastry flour
2 tsp. baking soda
1 tsp. salt
2 tsp. cinnamon
1 tsp. ground ginger
1/2 tsp. ground allspice
1 lb. (4 cups) sweet potatoes, peeled and grated

Blend oil and sugar together. Then add eggs, one at a time, beating after each addition. Combine dry ingredients and mix with egg mixture. Add grated sweet potatoes and mix well. Pour batter into two 9" round or one 13"x 9"x 2" pans. Bake at 350° for 40-50 minutes. Cool and frost.

TOFFEE CREAM CHEESE FROSTING

1/4 cup butter
1/2 cup brown sugar, packed
2 Tbs. strong coffee
1/2 tsp. vanilla
1 8 oz. pkg. cream cheese, softened
1/2 cup chopped walnuts

In a saucepan, melt butter, stir in brown sugar. Bring to a boil, stirring constantly. Stir in coffee, bring to a boil again. Remove from heat and stir in vanilla. Cool slightly and beat toffee into cream cheese. Frost cake and garnish with chopped nuts.

WHITE CHOCOLATE CAKE

1/4 pound white chocolate, grated
1/2 cup boiling water
1 cup butter, room temp.
2 cups sugar
4 eggs, separated
1 tsp. vanilla
2 1/2 cups cake flour
1 Tbs. baking powder
1 cup buttermilk
1 cup coconut
1 cup chopped nuts (walnuts or pecans)

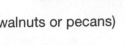

Melt chocolate in boiling water, then cool.

In a large bowl, cream butter and sugar then beat in egg yolks, one at a time, beating after each addition. Then add melted chocolate and vanilla. Sift flour and baking powder together and add alternately with buttermilk.

In a separate bowl, beat egg whites until stiff, then fold into the batter. Gently stir in coconut and nuts. Pour into three 9-inch round, greased and floured pans and bake at 350° for 40 minutes. Remove from pans, cool and frost.

FRENCH CREAM FROSTING

4 Tbs. flour
1 cup milk
1 1/4 tsp. vanilla
1/2 lb. butter (2 sticks)
1 cup superfine sugar

Mix flour and milk well and cook in a double boiler, stirring constantly, until thick as a pudding. Cover with waxed paper and cool to room temperature.

In a large bowl, cream butter and add pudding, mix well. Gradually add sugar and vanilla. Beat for 5 minutes with electric mixer. Frost cake, then garnish with sliced almonds.

SERIOUS POUND CAKE

This is the best pound cake you'll ever eat. It is rich and very fulfilling. One cake can be cut into 16 pieces. It is excellent with a fruit sauce or toasted with butter.

3 sticks butter or margarine
3 cups sugar
5 large eggs
3 cups cake flour
1 cup milk
2 tsp. fresh lemon juice
1 tsp. grated lemon zest

Cream butter, adding sugar gradually. Add eggs, one at a time, beating after each addition. Alternately add flour and milk. Then stir in lemon juice and zest. Bake in a tube pan (not a bundt pan) for one hour at 325° then increase temperature to 350° and bake another 30 minutes. Do not open oven during baking. Test with a knife for doneness.

RASPBERRY SAUCE

1 10 oz. pkg. frozen raspberries
1/4 cup powdered sugar
1 Tbs. Cointreau or orange flavored liquor
1 Tbs. orange juice

Thaw raspberries and blend in a food processor until smooth. Add remaining ingredients, process. Pour through a wire mesh strainer; press mixture with the back of a spoon to squeeze out liquid. Discard seeds. Spoon over individual servings of cake.

HAZELNUT CHEESECAKE

1 1/4 cup hazelnuts (filberts)
1/2 stick butter, melted
1 1/2 cups ground vanilla wafers or graham crackers
2 Tbs. sugar
3 8oz. pkgs. cream cheese, softened
1 cup sour cream
1 cup sugar
1/3 cup Frangelico or hazelnut-flavored liquor
1 tsp. vanilla extract
1/2 cup ground, toasted hazelnuts
6 large eggs

Preheat oven to 350°. Grind or chop 1 1/4 cups nuts and spread over a large cookie sheet. Bake for 8 - 10 minutes to toast them, being careful not to let them burn. Mix 3/4 cup nuts, cookie crumbs, butter and sugar and press into the bottom of a 10" springform pan.

For the filling, whip cream cheese and sour cream with an electric mixer until light and fluffy. Add sugar and beat well. Add liquor, vanilla and 1/2 cup hazelnuts then eggs, one at a time. Be sure to use the lowest speed of the mixer to keep air out of the batter. Pour into crust and bake for 55 minutes or until cake does not jiggle. Cool and store in refrigerator. This cake keeps well for several days.
Serves 10-16.

WHITE GRASS CHEESECAKE

1 1/2 cups vanilla wafer or graham cracker crumbs
5 Tbs. melted butter or margarine
1 Tbs. sugar
1/4 tsp. cinnamon
4 8 oz. pkgs. cream cheese, room temp.
1 cup sugar
6 eggs
1 tsp. vanilla

In a large bowl, mix cookie crumbs, margarine, 1 Tbs. sugar and cinnamon. Press into a 10-inch springform cake pan. Set aside.

Beat cream cheese with an electric mixer until smooth (use a high speed). Add sugar while mixing. Drop to a lower speed and add eggs, one at a time, mixing well. Stir in vanilla and pour into springform pan. Bake at 350° for 50 minutes or until cake is set. Cool, then refrigerate. Serve with fresh or frozen fruit. Delish.

Variation:

To make an amaretto flavored cake, simply add 1/4 cup Amaretto liquor and one additional egg.

> Sometimes this cake cracks - it is hard to avoid but you can hide it. We make our cakes gorgeous by decorating them with fresh fruit: strawberries, kiwi, mandarin oranges and blueberries. It's fun to make different designs.

WHITE CHOCOLATE CHEESECAKE

1 1/2 cups vanilla wafer crumbs
1/4 cup ground pecans
5 Tbs. butter or margarine, melted
12 oz. white chocolate
3 8 oz. pkg. cream cheese
1/2 cup sour cream
4 eggs
1 tsp. vanilla
1 11 oz. can mandarin oranges
1/4 cup Cointreau or other orange flavored liquor
1/2 cup orange juice
1 Tbs + 1 tsp. corn starch

Mix cookie crumbs, pecans and melted butter. Press into a 10-inch springform pan. Bake at 375° for 8 minutes.

Grate chocolate and melt in a double boiler, set aside.

In a large bowl, beat cream cheese and sour cream until soft. Add eggs one at a time, beating on low speed. Add vanilla and chocolate, stirring until well blended. Pour into pan and bake at 350° for 50 - 60 minutes, or until cake is set.

While cake is baking, drain oranges, saving 1/2 cup of liquid, and let them soak in Cointreau for about 30 minutes. Then combine Cointreau, 1/2 cup liquid, orange juice and cornstarch in a saucepan. Cook over medium heat until thick; cool. Arrange oranges on cooled cheesecake (it is fun to make designs) then spoon glaze over top. Refrigerate and enjoy.

> You can wow your friends with this beautiful cake
> It's a perfect party cake.

WALNUT PIE

This is a traditional pecan pie recipe. We choose to use walnuts. If you prefer pecans, indulge yourself.

3 eggs
1 1/2 cup chopped walnuts
1 1/2 tsp. vanilla
6 Tbs. melted butter or margarine
1 cup brown sugar
1 9-inch pie shell

In a bowl, mix eggs, nuts, vanilla, butter and sugar. Stir well and pour into pie shell. Bake 40 minutes at 350° or until pie is set. Cool and serve. Ice cream or whipped cream are an excellent accompaniment to this delicious dessert.

LAURIE'S APPLE PIE

8 medium baking apples
1 9-inch deep dish pie shell
1 tsp. cinnamon
3/4 cup softened margarine
3/4 cup rolled oats
3/4 cup brown sugar
3/4 cup whole wheat pastry flour
     or unbleached flour

Preheat oven to 350°. Pare and slice apples and toss with cinnamon. Pour apples into pie shell (they should be heaped above the crust). Mix margarine, oats, sugar and flour – kneading with your hands works best. Press on top of the apples, completely covering them. Bake for 50-60 minutes, or until top is browned and apples are soft when knife is inserted.

Delicious served warm with ice cream.
It's apple crisp in a pie shell!

KEY LIME PIE

It is important to use real key lime juice when making this pie. You can buy Nellie and Joe's Key Lime Juice in the grocery store.

1 1/4 cup graham cracker crumbs
1/3 cup melted butter or margarine
4 egg yolks
1 14 oz. can sweetened condensed milk
6 Tbs. Key lime juice (Key is the key)

Mix cracker crumbs and butter well and press into a 9-inch pie pan. In a bowl, mix egg yolks and sweetened milk. Add lime juice, a little at a time, stirring until smooth. Pour into crust and bake at 350° for 15 minutes. Chill and serve with whipped cream and Raspberry Sauce on page 169.

EASY CHOCOLATE
PEANUT BUTTER FUDGE

This recipe is from Carol McCormick.

1 cup butter, melted
1/2 cup peanut butter
1 pound (4 cups) confectioners sugar
1/2 cup cocoa powder
1 tsp. vanilla

Melt butter, mix in peanut butter. Mix sugar and cocoa together. Stir all ingredients together and press into a pan. Cool and cut.

MOCHA ESPRESSO FUDGE

1/4 cup butter
6 Tbs. cocoa powder
1/4 tsp. salt
1 pound confectioners sugar
1/4 cup brewed espresso coffee

Melt butter and cocoa in a saucepan. Stir in salt, sugar and coffee. Mix well. Drop onto wax paper and cool or refrigerate until served.

ALMOND FUDGE BROWNIES

Easy one pan mixing – a White Grass favorite!

2/3 cup margarine (1 stick + 3 Tbs.)
3/4 cup cocoa powder
2 cups sugar
4 eggs
1/2 tsp. almond extract
1/2 tsp. vanilla
1 1/4 cup unbleached white or all-purpose flour
1 tsp. baking powder
1 tsp. salt
1 cup chopped nuts – optional

Preheat oven to 350°. Grease and flour a 13 x 9 x 2 baking pan.

In a medium saucepan, melt margarine, then remove from heat. Add cocoa, sugar, eggs and vanilla, in that order, stirring after each addition. Then add remaining ingredients until just moistened. Spread into pan and bake 20 - 25 minutes.

Brownies are done if the center springs back when touched and edges pull away from pan. It may be difficult, but cool at least 20 minutes before cutting.

Our snow groomer, Barry, was helping in the kitchen one day, and accidentally put in the almond extract. We've done it that way ever since.

FRAZIER'S CHOCOLATE MOUSSE

5 oz. semisweet chocolate
3 Tbs. powdered sugar
4 1/2 Tbs. strong coffee
2 egg yolks
2 cups whipping cream

Melt chocolate over low heat in a saucepan. Stir in sugar, coffee and yolks – whip or stir until smooth. Remove from heat and cool at room temperature. Whip the cream with an electric mixer until stiff peaks form. Gently blend whipped cream and chocolate mixture. Spoon into serving bowls and chill. Makes 6-8 servings.

To make a Chocolate Mousse Pie, pour mousse into a prepared chocolate cookie crust and chill. Serve with whipped cream and chocolate shavings.

This is one of my favorite desserts, from one of my dearest friends, Frazier Hart Wilson. She won't admit it, but she is a great cook. MBG

BAKLAVA

This is a traditional Greek dessert, from my aunt, Betty Howell.   LKL

2 cups chopped walnuts
1 cup bread crumbs
1 Tbs. cinnamon
1 tsp. nutmeg
1/2 tsp. allspice
3/4 cup sugar
1 pound filo dough

Mix walnuts, breadcrumbs, spices and sugar to make a filling. Lay filo out on a flat surface. Butter two sheets at a time and lay 4 sheets in the bottom of a 9 x 13" pan. Spread some filling over the dough. Keep piling up dough (2 sheets) and filling, leaving 4 sheets of dough for the top. Don't forget to keep buttering the filo. Bake at 350° until light brown, cool. Then pour syrup (below) over the top.

Syrup

1 1/2 cup sugar
2 cups water
1 1/2 tsp. cinnamon plus 2 cinnamon sticks
1 tsp. lemon juice
1/2 cup honey

Cook together sugar, water, cinnamon and lemon juice until it thickens. Then add honey and heat until it boils. Remove from heat and cool. Pour over cool baklava and let soak in. Cut from corner to corner to form small diamond shaped pieces.

PECAN TARTS

Dough:

      1 stick margarine or butter
      1 3 oz. package cream cheese
      1 cup flour

Filling:

      1 1/4 cup brown sugar
      2 eggs
      3 Tbs. melted butter
      1/2 tsp. vanilla
      3/4 cup chopped pecans

Mix all dough ingredients, kneading with your hands, refrigerate while you make the filling. Then divide dough into 12 balls and press into small muffin tins. Spoon in filling 3/4 of the way full. Bake until golden at 350° for 30 minutes.

This is one of our all-time favorite desserts. Not only are the tarts delicious, but they look beautiful on a tray of holiday cookies. A tin of tarts makes a fabulous gift.

FRUIT COBBLER

1/2 cup butter or margarine
1/2 cup sugar
1 cup flour
3 cups berries or fruit*
1/4 tsp. nutmeg (optional)

To make topping, allow butter to soften to room temperature. Using a fork, mix in sugar then flour in a bowl until you have a crumbly mixture.

Pour berries into a 8" square or 9" round glass baking dish. Sprinkle topping over berries and nutmeg on top. Bake at 375° for 30 minutes or until topping is golden. Don't forget to serve with vanilla ice cream.

*This cobbler can be made with any fruit or combination. For instance:

apples	raspberries
peaches	blueberries
blackberries	cherries

There's nothing better than picking fresh fruit for a homemade cobbler. If you are lucky enough to live around wild berries, freeze some so, in the dead of winter, you can enjoy a taste of summer.

A Word From The Dolly Sods Lama

When our staff gets excited about winter and starting up White Grass, the entire thing becomes highlighted in knowing how well fed we will be. Appetites are heightened through many long cold hours out there, and nothing is more nourishing than the café's fare. As their worst critic, they've never let us down.

Keep a skier well fed and they will enjoy more trails, more often, and travel farther. In January, after a long trek, there is an easy way to one's heart...through their hunger. This cookbook and a winter season at White Grass is proof of that! Knowing at trails end this fine cuisine awaits, creates an easy way to enjoy your work and play. I am one of the world's most energetic and excited nordic skiers, and I credit all of it to Laurie and Mary Beth's balanced cooking.

The sweet smells of soup, garlic, and fresh pies greet you upon entering White Grass. May you have the energy and time to enjoy some of our winter's magic and build up a cross country's appetite for these wonderful recipes. If you ever get wandering along some of the windy West Virginia's roads in winter, do stop in to visit us. Mmmm good food will enter your mind when you open the door.

Chip Chase,
March 2000

I N D E X

184

Some Of Our Favorite Suppliers

Frankferd Farms Foods
717 Saxonburg Blvd.
Saxonburg, PA 16056
412-352-9500
412-352-9510 fax

Excellent quality fresh milled
organic flours, grains, beans,
pancake mixes, granola and
other natural foods.

Frontier Cooperative Herbs
P.O. Box 299
Norway, IA 52318
1-800-669-3275
1-800-717-HERB fax

Excellent quality herbs and
spices free from chemical
pesticides and radiation.

Mountain Aquaculture and
Producers Assoc., Inc.
P.O. Box 12
Parsons, WV 26287
304-478-6272

Smoked trout shipped in dry ice.
Also gift boxes with smoked trout,
West Va. honey, maple syrup or
berry jam.

Stan Evans Bakery
1417 Grandview Ave.
Columbus, OH 43212
614-4486-4414

Mail order whole grain sliced
bread - 2-pound loaves. (We use
the light wheat for sandwiches at
the cafe).

Bon Appétit!

To order more cookbooks,
send $12.95 + $2.50 shipping and handling
per copy to:

White Grass Cafe
HC 70 Box 299
Davis, WV 26260
(304)-866-4114

Visit our website at
www.whitegrass.com
Send us email at
chip@whitegrass.com

White Grass Cafe Cookbook Order Form
Send check or credit card number.

🍎•🍎•🍎•🍎•🍎•🍎•🍎•🍎•🍎•🍎•🍎•🍎•🍎•🍎•🍎•🍎

Number of Copies_____

Name_____

Address_____

City/State/Zip_____

Phone_____

Credit Card Number
_____

Exp. Date_____

Signature_____

Cookbooks can also be ordered at www.amazon.com